W9-CQT-480

STOLEN
CHILDHOOD

GARFINKLE
ESTATE

'Love does not dominate, it cultivates'

For Ruth, who died aged 12
but not unheard

STOLEN CHILDHOOD

In Search of the Rights of the Child

Anuradha Vittachi

Polity Press

in association with North-South Productions Ltd
and Channel Four Television Company Limited

Copyright © North-South Productions Ltd

First published 1989 by Polity Press
in association with Basil Blackwell

Editorial office:
Polity Press, 65 Bridge Street,
Cambridge CB2 1UR, UK

Marketing and production:
Basil Blackwell Ltd
108 Cowley Road, Oxford OX4 1JF, UK

Basil Blackwell Inc.
3 Cambridge Center,
Cambridge, MA 02142, USA

All rights reserved. Except for the quotation of short passages for the purposes of criticism and review, no part of this publication may be reproduced, stored in a retrieval system, or transmitted, in any form or by any means, electronic, mechanical, photocopying, recording or otherwise, without the prior permission of the publisher.

Except in the United States of America, this book is sold subject to the condition that it shall not, by way of trade or otherwise, be lent, resold, hired out, or otherwise circulated without the publisher's prior consent in any form of binding or cover other than that in which it is published and without a similar condition including this condition being imposed on the subsequent purchaser.

ISBN 0 7456 0714 4
ISBN 0 7456 0720 9 (pbk)

British Library Cataloguing in Publication Data

A CIP catalogue record for this book is available from the British Library.

Library of Congress Cataloging-in-Publication Data

A CIP catalogue record for this book is available from the Library of Congress.

Typeset in 10 on 12pt Sabon by Oxprint Ltd, Aristotle Lane, Oxford
Printed in Great Britain by Scotprint Ltd, Musselburgh

CONTENTS

FOREWORD
SIR RICHARD ATTENBOROUGH

Not so long ago, I became a grandfather for the first time. Like all new grandparents, my wife and I worried throughout our daughter's pregnancy that something might go wrong. Because we were travelling a great deal, the knowledge that Jane, in London, had access to every possible medical care was an enormous comfort. Our grandson, Sam, a healthy eight-pounder with two of everything in the right place, was born in June 1984 and since then two more grandchildren have arrived on the scene.

In the summer of 1987 all three of them spent a holiday with us. And as I watched and held them, marvelling at their strong limbs and, on occasion, even stronger lungs, I found myself reflecting on how fortunate they were. If one was taken ill, for example, we knew that medical help was always at hand. We also knew that they had been born of healthy mothers; that, come what may, they would not go short of nourishment; that immunization was a matter of course; and that as they grew older, they would receive support and help from the family, would benefit from sound education and would be protected from danger.

Inevitably then, I started to reflect on the lives of other children, in other parts of the world – lives glimpsed during my travels as a film-maker and latterly as one of UNICEF's Goodwill Ambassadors. How must it feel, I thought, to be the parents or grandparents of a child dying before your very eyes? To have no doctor, no medication, no food, and, through lack of basic health education, no knowledge of what to do. To have no escape from the poverty trap and to hold no hope for the future. And yet for millions of people, particularly in the developing world, this nightmare is a constant reality.

Last year alone, some 14 million children under the age of five died in developing countries. That's one in three of all deaths. The major causes of this appalling figure – almost incomprehensible in its magnitude – are diarrhoea, measles, tetanus, whooping cough, polio, acute respiratory infections and, of course, under nutrition. Diseases and conditions which are largely preventable and which we in industrialized countries have all but eradicated. Diseases and conditions that can and must be defeated throughout the world. All it would take is health care, costing unbelievably little, and simple education of parents in its use. The political will to act collectively, internationally, could prevent this shocking and unnecessary loss of life.

It was this so-called 'silent emergency', together with the realization that children everywhere are increasingly at risk from violence, war, abuse, drugs and exploitation, that motivated me to devote a part of my time each year to UNICEF. The part I can play in promoting these issues, is, of course, very small. However, we should not, I am certain, under-estimate the impact that we as individual parents and citizens can have collectively on policy. When confronted by statistics like those I have mentioned, we tend to find ourselves overwhelmed by the sheer scale of the crisis. We feel helpless, impotent, and may believe we should leave it to the politicians – as some do, perhaps, on hearing about worldwide environmental problems.

But we should not forget that it is individuals who shape the policies of governments and it is precisely due to the actions of individuals – political leaders, scientists, journalists, artists and, of course, voters – that we are now seeing a shift towards 'green politics' in Europe and elsewhere. Ultimately, I'm sure, the transformation of global attitudes necessary to bring about a revolution in child welfare will also happen through a similar mobilization of world opinion.

I believe that this book and the television series to which it relates will play a tremendously important part in raising people's awareness of child-related issues and motivating them to take action. At the heart of the book is the concept of children's rights, first defined 30 years ago in the United Nations Declaration on the Rights of the Child and now being given legal force by means of a UN Convention embodying a specific set of standards to which all signatory states will be expected to adhere.

In STOLEN CHILDHOOD we meet children whose rights, as defined in the Convention, have been abused, neglected or endangered; an Indian child, suffering from polio; an abandoned street child in New York City; a mentally disabled teenager in Sweden; the children of Philippine prostitutes and many, many more. Through their lives, we learn not only about the needs and rights of children but also about the obligations of adults – at parental, national and international levels. And we learn, too, of the vital significance of the Convention on the Rights of the Child.

The Convention is desperately important, first of all, because it gives legal weight to the acknowledgement that children have specific human rights. It includes 35 articles covering civil, political, economic, social and cultural rights, based on three principles: that children need special safeguards beyond those provided for adults; that the best environment for a child's survival and development is within the family; and that governments and the adult world should act in the best interests of children. Countries that formally accept and sign the Convention will have the responsibility of adapting their own domestic laws and regulations to meet these provisions.

In addition, the Convention provides a conceptual framework within which public support can be mobilized. It sets standards in child welfare which all countries are expected to attain or surpass, as well as global targets such as the vaccination of every child in the world and the control and eventual eradication of child labour. Within this framework, a practical course of action can be planned within a known budget. And when action becomes practicable, public support must surely be forthcoming in order to ensure that it is implemented.

The time has come to share internationally the information we have on the welfare of children, to bring these proposals to everyone's attention and to pool our resources to achieve the necessary shift in global attitudes. When we have attained these objectives, charity and sentimentality, which so frequently motivate our present response to children's needs, will no longer be necessary, adequate or tolerable.

The Convention on the Rights of the Child can be our greatest legacy to the future of mankind, our gift to succeeding generations of children and grandchildren. By spurring each and every country to accept and implement basic human rights for children, no matter where in the world they happen to be born, we can create a yardstick against which adult behaviour will continue to be judged for ever more.

We stand, I believe, on the threshold of a new era. It is within our power – as never before in history – to shoulder a collective responsibility for the welfare of all children in all circumstances in all countries. This is now a matter of great urgency. The necessary international structures and network of communications are already in place. All it needs now is political will. And courage.

Sir Richard Attenborough CBE
UNICEF Goodwill Ambassador

ACKNOWLEDGEMENTS

The author, North-South Productions and Polity Press would especially like to thank UNICEF for their full cooperation and support without which the publication of this book would not have been possible. It should be pointed out, however, that the views expressed are those of the author alone and do not necessarily reflect those of UNICEF or any other organization. UNICEF cannot be held responsible, therefore, for any criticism of individuals or governments expressed in the text.

This book is based on the television series *Stolen Childhood*, produced by North-South Productions in conjunction with Channel 4 (UK), NRK (Norway), SVT 1 (Sweden), RAI 1 (Italy), RTVE (Spain), Asterisk Productions, TV Ontario and ACCESS Alberta (Canada) and The Discovery Channel (USA).

The producers would also like to thank the following organizations for their support: Redd Barna, the Save the Children Alliance, Rädda Barnen, the Canadian International Development Agency (CIDA), the Department of Justice, Canada, the Canadian Public Health Association, the Spanish Red Cross Society, the Italian Commitee for UNICEF, the Royal Norwegian Ministry of Development (NORAD), the Norwegian Ministry of Justice and the Norwegian Ministry of Consumer Affairs.

AUTHOR'S ACKNOWLEDGEMENTS

My thanks are due first of all to the children who appear in this book. I hope, like them, that making their experiences known will help the millions of other children for whom they are ambassadors. Thanks are due next to the many unsung adults who work for children, sometimes in situations of personal danger; without the information they have collected about the reality of children's lives, this book could not have been written.

Special thanks are due to Peter Stalker and Peter Armstrong for looking over drafts of the manuscript with care beyond the call of duty; and my gratitude to everyone at *New Internationalist* for their love and concern, especially Wendy Slack and Debbie Taylor for their warm support. I would also like to thank everyone at North-South Productions, Richard Keefe for following his intuition, Veronique Seifert for her efficiency, Charlotte Bannister for her enthusiasm and both Shana Magraw and Patricia Lee for their work on the photographs.

Neither this book nor anything else that I have written in the past decade would have materialized but for two people: Tarzie Vittachi and Peter Adamson. Their ideas have been formative and their words inspiring: many re-appear on these pages. And without Chris Robertson, I might have been tempted only to react in horror at the sight of suffering children and recite a list of their miseries. For transmuting these sights (which are paralysing) into insights (which are activating), I have Christ to thank.

I would also like to thank the film-makers and researchers who made the television series that stands side by side with this book; thanks are also due to John Gibb and to Nick Hedley, Robin Skynner and Sheila Kitzinger for their wisdom about mothers and babies.

Most of all, though, I must thank my children and step-children, who never complained while I devoted my time over the past few months to writing about other children. On the contrary, they read drafts, did the laundry, cooked dinners, brought me cups of tea — and left me in guilt-free peace to write. No writer has been treated better.

Anuradha Vittachi
Hedgerley Wood
April 1989

AUTHOR'S NOTE

A child can be a girl or a boy – but to say 'he/she' and 'hers or his' makes for such a clumsy text that I have chosen another way out of this dilemma. Sometimes I have referred to a child as 'she' and at other times as 'he': the choice is usually random.

How to refer to large and disparate areas of the world in generalized terms also presents problems. Some people are upset by 'the Third World' and others by 'developing countries'. Should Europe and North America combined be referred to as 'the West' or as 'the North'? In despair, I have used a variety of terms, though I have favoured what seems to me the simplest and most meaningful: 'poor countries' and 'rich countries'.

THE CONVENTION ON THE RIGHTS OF THE CHILD

The Convention on the Rights of the Child – a set of international standards and measures which signatory countries agree to adopt and to incorporate in their laws – has been drafted by the UN Commission on Human Rights. This treaty recognizes the particular vulnerability of children and brings together in one comprehensive code the benefits and protection for children scattered in scores of other agreements.

The Convention's aim is to set standards for the defence of children against the neglect and abuse they face to varying degrees in all countries every day. It is careful to allow for the different cultural, political and material realities among states and places special emphasis on the primary caring and protective responsibility of the family. It also stresses the need for legal and other protection of the child, before and after birth, and the vital role of international cooperation in achieving the realization of children's rights.

The guiding spirit of the document is always the best interests of the child.

Here in summary form, are some highlights of the Convention:

- Children are defined as those under the age of 18, unless national laws fix an earlier age of majority.

- Every child has the inherent right to life, and States shall ensure to the maximum child survival and development.

- Every child has the right to a name and nationality from birth.

- When courts, welfare institutions or administrative authorities deal with children, the child's best interests shall be a primary consideration. The child's opinions shall be given careful consideration.

- States shall ensure that each child enjoys full rights without discrimination or distinctions of any kind.

- Children shall not be separated from their parents, unless by competent authorities for their well-being; States should facilitate reunification of families by permitting travel in or out of their borders.

- Parents have the primary responsibility for a child's upbringing, but States shall provide them with appropriate assistance and develop child-care institutions.

- States shall provide parentless children with suitable alternative care. The adoption process shall be carefully regulated and international agreements should be sought to provide safeguards and assure legal validity if and when adoptive parents intend to move the child from his or her country of birth.

- Disabled children shall have the right to special treatment, education and care.

- The child is entitled to the highest attainable standard of health. States shall ensure that health care is provided to all children, placing emphasis on preventive measures, health education and reduction of infant mortality.

- Primary education shall be free and compulsory as early as possible; discipline should respect the child's dignity. Education should prepare the child for life in a spirit of understanding, peace and tolerance.

- Children shall have time to rest and play and equal opportunities for cultural and artistic activities.

- States shall protect the child from economic exploitation and work that may interfere with education or be harmful to health and well-being.

- States shall protect children from the illegal use of drugs and involvement in drug production or trafficking.

- All efforts shall be made to eliminate the abduction and trafficking of children.

- Capital punishment or life imprisonment shall not be imposed for crimes committed before the age of 18. Children in detention should be separated from adults; they must not be tortured or suffer cruel or degrading treatment.

- No child shall take any part in hostilities; children exposed to armed conflict shall receive special protection.

- Children of minority and indigenous populations shall freely enjoy their own culture, religion and language.

- Children who have suffered maltreatment, neglect or detention should receive appropriate treatment or training for recovery and rehabilitation.

- States should make the Convention's rights widely known to both adults and children and undertake the legislative and administrative measures necessary for their implementation.

I

THE BETRAYAL OF CHILDHOOD

I suppose that the chief thing about being a child is being in the power of grown-ups. Everything comes from them – food, laws, treats and punishments. They have the power to give and to withhold. Some of them make up the rules as they go along to suit their convenience and the child, who would like the chance to make up a few rules himself, knows it.

The World of Childhood

In May 1986, a unique conference was held in Brazil. The conference location was unusual – it was held in the capital's central park – and so was the choice of delegates: it was a conference on street children arranged by street children themselves. To get there, 432 children had travelled for days by bus, train, and on foot, from every part of Brazil.

One of the few adults invited to the meeting, Peter Taçon of Childhope, was very impressed. 'It was a new experience for [adults] to listen rather than talk,' he said. 'The children spoke calmly, easily, mostly in an organized way, chairing the conference themselves.'

When the conference delegates visited Congress Hall to put their questions to politicians, one girl, Carmen, looked around her in surprise at the beautiful paintings and furniture – and then at her own dirty, worn out clothes in the midst of luxury. Her question was direct: 'How could someone build and live in such surroundings when children are starving to death outside?'

Carmen was right. The painful truth is that children are 'starving to death outside' – and that we allow them to do so. For most adults, the experience of watching a child die before their eyes, feeling powerless to help that child back to life, must be one of the most painful experiences imaginable. If there were any way they could save that child's life, they would surely do it. And yet more than a million children each month fade away unnecessarily from hunger-exacerbated diseases. A child dies every two seconds: in the time it takes to read this sentence, another child will have died. And we allow it to happen. How can we reconcile these two realities?

EVERYBODY'S CHILDREN

That adults see children as very precious is taken for granted. An advertisement on a hoarding near my local railway station consists of a single line of text, 'For the most fantastic news in the history of the world', captioning a photograph of two old ladies and a young couple sitting on a park bench –

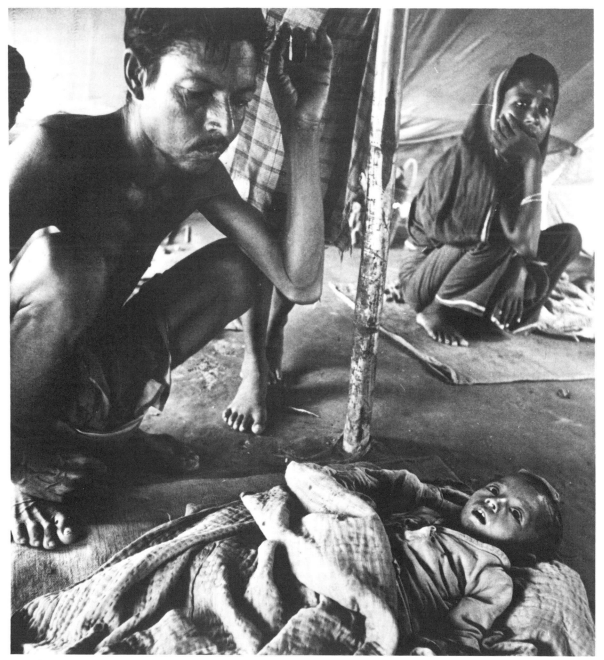

A Pakistani father watches over his dying son. Children already weakened by malnutrition are easy prey to pneumonia and diarrhoeal diseases.

and evidently the young woman has whispered to the young man something that has made him punch the air above him in a whoop of celebration. The advertisers can rely even on a person glimpsing the advertisement from a passing bus, as I did, to be able to understand that the cryptic reference to 'the most fantastic news in the history of the world' must mean the couple were going to have a baby.

Nevertheless there remains a fatal gap between the loving protection adults promise to children and the experience they actually offer. Why do we betray the children who die unnecessarily every other second? It may be that we offer protection only to the children whose needs we see with acute immediacy – children whom we identify as our own. The politicians at Congress Hall addressed by Carmen probably looked after their own children at home with great care, even though they failed to honour Carmen's simplest needs for food and shelter, for Carmen is someone else's child. Her needs are invisible.

But as the world shrinks, and we receive sophisticated media images of children suffering in other parts of the world, some of that parochialism is beginning to disappear. More adults are beginning to 'see' children everywhere – and with this awakening perception comes a more widespread sense that all children should be protected, not just those belonging to our own family or tribal group.

CHANGING PRIORITIES

But reaching out to children around the world is not easy. How do we touch a child to comfort him if he is 5,000 miles away? How do we feed a girl who is hungry on the other side of the planet? How do we change the situation of tens of thousands of children faced with hunger, illiteracy, war? Both the distance and the scale of the problems induce despair. Many of us try to break through the barrier of defeat and resignation by putting money in the collection boxes of organizations like Oxfam or Save the Children Fund, hoping that they will know better than we how to reach the children whose names we don't know. And still others of us join organizations that link our family to a family in a poverty-stricken village, so that our sense of 'who belongs' can be stretched to include others.

But these actions, we know, are drops in an ocean. How are children in their millions to be helped – and how are poor families to be freed from the misery of depending on the loose change of charity? Is it even possible? It seems clear that it will only be possible if there are changes beyond the scope of individuals or voluntary organizations. The powers that run the world could make a difference – governments, for example, or commercial giants like the richest banks or multinational companies: but it seems naïve to hope that people running such institutions are going to shift their eyes far from the columns that tell them of profit-and-loss and turn their gaze to the rights of children.

As Carmen pointed out, there is money available to build beautiful buildings and furnish them luxuriously. Not everyone lives on the street in worn out clothes as she does. Will the people who have access to large amounts of money care about Carmen enough to see her as a human person with the right to live and learn and contribute to society? Or will they see her only as a beggar in the street out to pick their pockets?

There is money also to buy armaments that cost the world some $900 billion each year. And before we despair about feeding so many hungry children we should take in the fact that there is already enough food grown to feed everyone alive: children do not go hungry in a barren world but one where butter mountains swelter and surplus wheat is set on fire. Further, UNICEF, the chief United Nations agency for the care and protection of children, says that each one of the 14 million sick children who die unnecessarily every year could be saved by remedies that would cost us only loose change. The problem lies not in an absolute shortage of money or food or remedies for sick children. It lies elsewhere: in the lack of priority given by adults to the basic human rights of children.

James Grant, head of UNICEF, has pointed out that,

Whereas most nations can and do produce up-to-date quarterly statistics on the health of their economies, few nations can produce even annual statistics on the health of their children.

This failure to monitor the effects of economic and social change on the well-being of the most vulnerable . . . is both a cause and a symptom of the lack of political priority afforded to this task. Yet there could be no more important test for any government than the test of whether or not it is protecting the nation's vulnerable and whether or not it is protecting the nation's future – and its children are both.

So although politicians are fond of saying that children are 'our most precious investment', they seem to keep very few tabs on this investment. Is it because they don't really see, sharply, the truth of the words they speak?

THE CONVENTION ON THE RIGHTS OF THE CHILD

Now, however, children are at last coming into focus. Not only are more individuals and groups joining an organically growing network around the world that supports children's rights, but governments are beginning to respond.

Forty of these governments have been sending

Vietnamese children with mortar bombs: the world spends more on arms and luxuries than on child health programmes.

Unemployed father in Madrid: a child has the right to survival, protection and development.

delegates to the United Nations for one week a year for ten years, beginning in the Year of the Child in 1979, to help draft an international agreement that lays down the minimum rights that every child in the world should have. These include the basic rights necessary for survival and development – the right, for example, to an adequate standard of living, to health care, to education; it also includes the child's right to stay with his family if it has the child's best interests at heart – and to be cared for elsewhere if the family is abusive; it includes the child's right to protection from exploitation through child labour, through being kidnapped and sold, or through sexual abuse. And it includes the child's right to her own identity: not only to have a name and nationality, but to have privacy and dignity, and a voice in decisions that concern her life.

This agreement is known as the 'Convention on the Rights of the Child'. There is already a UN 'Declaration on the Rights of the Child' signed in 1959: but while the Declaration has only moral force, the Convention is legally binding. Once agreed and signed, the rights of a child as delineated in the Convention will have the force of law in the countries whose governments have signed the document. And the 40 governments that are expected to sign the agreement at the end of 1989 are, the UN hopes, just the fore-runners. Eventually, all other governments in the world may agree to sign.

The more countries sign the Convention, of course, the more weight it will carry as a genuine expression of an international consensus. If and when every government signs it, there will, at last, be a universal minimum standard for children's rights – a standard that would not only reflect but reinforce a raised political awareness that children should have basic human rights. A well-supported Convention could become a major instrument for legitimizing the concept of children's rights.

People who have been campaigning for children's rights would then be able to stop using their energies to persuade their governments that children's rights are a sensible and necessary idea, and use those energies instead to make sure the governments are actually putting their promise to honour children's rights into practice. In other words, the case that children need rights will have been won – and the burden of proof can be switched from those who want children to have rights to those who must now demonstrate how well they are honouring those rights. A successful Convention could, therefore, mark a major shift in political consciousness, with the rights of children placed firmly on the political agenda; and children may at last stop being relegated to invisibility.

THE IMPORTANCE OF PUBLIC OPINION

But that success depends on how far public indignation is mobilized against the injustices done to children – for international laws cannot be enforced in domestic courts as national laws are: the government and the people must see and feel the rightness of these international laws if they are to make sure they are enforced in their own country by the pressure of their focused will. What will make people feel strongly enough about children and their rights – what will galvanize them into putting pressure on governments?

An answer may be found in the better relationships that adults have with some children, usually children they know well. When an adult looks at such a child with clear eyes and feels, vividly, her reality as a human being, a being both vulnerable and full of potent life, then it is not difficult for that adult to act in defence of that child's rights, and to insist on others acting in the same spirit. But can the quality of this relationship be replicated in the relationship between such an adult and the children of the world?

The crucial factor remains the willingness in the adult to be open to a heartfelt connectedness. When that connectedness is present, we have no difficulty in being motivated to act, or to think of ways to help. So what breaks our connection? What separates us?

Partly it is a matter of geography. We simply don't know the facts about the lives of children far away, though books like this one and films and television programmes are doing more and more to bring us news about children everywhere. Partly it is a matter of the tribalism in our usual sources of information and in our own minds, which means that we are not used to thinking of the whole world as our tribal group. But there is also another, subtler barrier.

An adult, even a habitually caring one, may turn his eyes away from the child whose pain reminds him too much of his own: the child whose disabled body reminds him of his own fears of exclusion and abandonment by 'normal' society; the child whose emaciated body or ragged clothes evoke his own fears of destitution and death; the baby whose bewildered cries remind him of his own helplessness and unanswered tears when he was an infant. For an adult to look at the lives of children in pain requires courage, because it also means facing his own pain. It can seem easier to turn quickly away.

And yet we must look; we must see. For until we see, children will continue to suffer at our unseeing hands – and at the hands of those adults whose hearts are so shut off from the human reality of children that they see them only as objects to exploit. As long as we deny the full experience of the pain within us, we will protect ourselves from becoming fully aware of the pain outside; in one way or another we will deny its existence or its nature, and disempower our ability to make a difference. We may fool ourselves, for instance, that the 'problem' lies 'out there', beyond our scope, when the problem really lies in our unwillingness to make a truly open-hearted connection to children everywhere as if they were our own.

EXPLOITING CHILDREN'S ENERGIES

In this book we will begin to see something of the situation of children around the world – seeing, for instance, that between 50 and 150 million children are bound by adults to a lifetime of manual labour that starts when they are only eight, or six, or even just four years old. Work in itself is not necessarily harmful – schoolwork, after all, is work, and children are expected to work hard at school. But the conditions in which millions of children are expected to work are reminiscent of the worst days of nineteenth-century industrialization. In Peru, children are sent down mines; in Rome, they are forced to pick pockets for modern-day Fagins; Frederick Engels's description of conditions in a nineteenth-century

Children are exploited as labourers today just as they were in the nineteenth century.

glassworks could easily substitute for one in India today:

In the manufacture of glass, the hard labour, the irregularity of the hours, the frequent night-work, and especially the great heat of the working place (100 to 130 Fahrenheit) engender in children general debility and disease, stunted growth, and especially affections of the eye, bowel complaints, and rheumatic and bronchial affections. Many of the children are pale, have red eyes, often blind for weeks at a time, suffer from violent nausea, vomiting, coughs, colds and rheumatism. When the glass is withdrawn from the fire, the children must often go into such heat that the boards on which they stand catch fire under their feet. The glassblowers usually die young of debility and chest infections.

Despite all these hours of work, the children are paid so badly, if at all, that they have no means of earning their way out of exploitation.

Nor are children guaranteed safety within the bosom of the family. Most children who are sexually abused are assaulted not by strangers in dark alleys but at home by people they know and depend on. Only 11 per cent of children who were sexually abused, according to one Western survey, were abused by strangers. The child's developing sexuality, which the family is supposed to protect from violation, is consumed by the family. Other children are abused by physical violence or neglect from their parents. Three children a day are estimated to die of abuse at the hands of their parents in the United States. Millions of children cannot trust the adults in their own households for a minimum standard of safe care.

Children who leave home to escape family violence confront violence on the streets. Street children who sell newspapers or peanuts without a licence, or sell their sexuality as prostitutes in order to survive, are liable to arrest by police who regularly blackmail the children into giving them their earnings or performing sexual acts in return for setting them free. These children are vulnerable not only to predators like these police but even to exterminators: the Independent Commission on International Humanitarian Issues (ICIHI) reports that, 'In one large South American city, officially-licensed radio stations have openly urged private individuals to do away with street children physically. The result reportedly is not only widespread violence but the actual killing of two youngsters, on average, every day. . . . They can die, and no one will notice.'

The exploitation of children is not a rare aberration, the work of a few psychopathic monsters. It is regular and institutionalized in the factories that depend on cheap child labour, in the schools that educate children not in order to develop the children's minds but in order to shape them to fit the needs of the country's industrial system, and in the families that consume a child's sexuality by appealing to fear or family loyalty.

A healthy, well-loved child has abundant, exuberant energy. But these energies can be stolen. Instead of being safe-guarded and channelled for the sake of a child's own, unique, human development, they may be robbed from the child and used mechanically as fuel for someone else's purposes. The stealing of children's energies is robbery with violence on a vast scale. And when adults allow such robberies to take place, they are betraying the power of protection entrusted to them.

PAWNS IN WAR

Perhaps the worst example of child exploitation comes with the willingness of adults to use children in war – even using warplanes to drop bombs shaped like pretty toys in order to attract children. When a child picks up one of these bombs, it explodes. These bombs were designed deliberately to destroy children because children are precious to parents; one set of adults had concluded that hurting children is the most effective form of terrorism conducted against another set of adults.

Palestinian refugee children captured by Israelis have had their bones broken before being returned to their parents. Defence for Children International estimates that in South Africa more than 1,000 children have been shot by police as a result of the government's policy of terrorizing children. A further 10,000 children have been detained without trial.

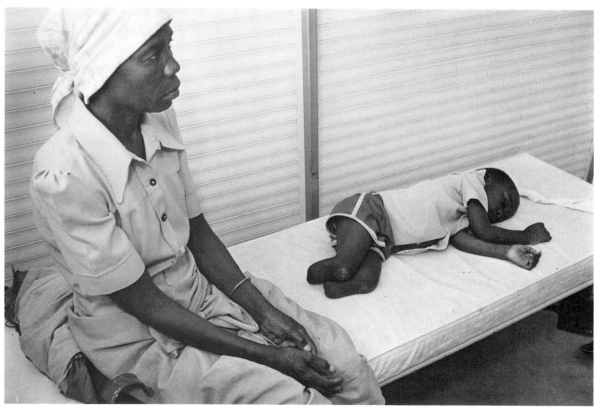

Child victim in Mozambique, his feet blown away by a mine planted by South African-backed Renamo guerrillas.

Says paediatrician Dr Nkosazana Zuma, of the Health and Refugee Trust of South Africa (HEART):

There are no words to describe meeting a child who has been tortured in a South African prison. One boy attended a funeral of two school friends who had been shot dead by the police – and was himself arrested, beaten up and given electric shocks. He was then kept in solitary confinement for three weeks. 'I was crying and just sitting,' he says, while prison officers ate the food brought for him by his mother. When he was released, his ears where bleeding. He says: 'After my release, I could not stand it. Every night I would hear gunshots. You cannot learn or do anything.'

In Mozambique, where South African-backed rebels are attempting to destabilize the government, children are forced to collaborate. A report from War-on-Want, a British agency working on behalf of the poor, describes how 12-year-old José was asked by rebel troops who had entered his village whether his father was a member of the local militia. Fearful for his father's safety, José denied it. But the rebels 'stormed through the village until they found and killed his father. As a punishment to José for trying to save his father, they mutilated him, cutting off parts of his fingers and one of his ears.' On a later raid on the village, they kidnapped José as a 'recruit'.

As Katerina Tomsevski and Nigel Cantwell write in their study of children's rights, 'There is no form of [state] repression from which children have been spared. Torture, "disappearances", summary executions, unacknowledged detention, deaths in custody . . .'

Children are also exploited directly by states in armed combat as child soldiers. Participation in combat is a brutal and brutalizing experience. Recent reports on the effects of the Vietnam war on American soldiers show how profoundly the adult soldiers remain scarred, 20 years on: child soldiers cannot be expected to remain unaffected by their experiences. The *National Catholic Reporter* describes the psychology of child soldiers in

In the 1980s, child soldiers have played an increasing role in the world's many conflicts.

Guatemala: '[They are] products of a culture of violence which has seemingly anaesthetized them to the terror of war. Young and impressionable, they are susceptible to ideologies of any side, and they are eager to use their guns.'

In most countries, young people may not marry or drive until they are around 18 years of age; they cannot vote at least until then – and these restrictions are accepted by most adults as common sense. After all, children should not be allowed to make major decisions that could seriously affect their lives or that of others, when they are so inexperienced in life or too irresponsible. And yet the state may consider this same child, who is apparently too inexperienced to vote, to be experienced enough to go to war to kill another human being or be killed himself.

SLAVERY AND EMANCIPATION

Children have no political power outside the home – adults hold it on their behalf – and very little inside it. By defining children as weak and vulnerable, irrational and irresponsible (or even, sometimes, as angelically pure and innocent), adults justify the position of power they hold over children, very much as husbands used to justify their power over wives or paternalistic slave-owners over their slaves.

Martin Hoyles has observed drily: 'Indignation is often expressed that women or blacks are treated like children, but not so often that children are treated the way they are.' Adults have control over virtually everything that a child does, from the moment the child wakes up in the morning to the moment the child goes to bed; and most adults feel entitled to that control – which might even seem justifiable if children were well cared for as a result. But the danger of absolute power is that it can easily be misused and, as we have seen, the exercise of adult power over children's lives has meant deprivation or active exploitation for tens of millions of children.

State authorities in Italy offer an example of the injustice that can follow when parental power over children is unbridled:

There are abandoned children in institutions whom nobody comes to see for years on end, but when we finally make out the adoption papers we are advised of the opposition of the parents, who remember the existence of the children solely for the purpose of claiming proprietory rights. 'I don't look after him, but he is mine.' . . . If the child is 'their own property' they can do with it what they like, they use it as they think fit and any approach by the authorities is regarded as an interference by them.

The abandoned children in these cases are slaves to the whims of their parents. They do not have the legal right to live with an adoptive family even though they are utterly neglected by their own, for no reason other than that they are children. Such children are slaves not because their lives are so tragic, but because they are bereft of their own rights. Slaves were sometimes treated benevolently by their owners but that didn't stop them being slaves: slavery ended only when slaves gained rights of their own as free citizens – when they were no

longer at the mercy of their owners' sense of obligation to treat a slave well, or not bother. In the same way, a child will only be free of slavery to state or parent when children's rights are legalized.

Children have no political power because adults do not allow them to have it. We keep that power for ourselves, and so children must trust us to protect them with our political decisions. But, as we have seen, we often betray that trust: we betray their vulnerability by failing to protect them – and we betray their power by not letting them speak up and act on their own behalf. Like the wolf who disguises himself as Little Red Riding Hood's grandmother, too many adults disarm children in the guise of kind protector – and then, treacherously, exploit them.

THE CLOAK OF INVISIBILITY

But Little Red Riding Hood is beginning to emerge from under her hooded cloak: we are beginning to see her face. Some adults, of course, notably mothers, have always known their children well and seen their care as a priority. But adults like this who devote themselves to children often find themselves pulled under the same cloak of invisibility as children do.

Motherhood, like childhood, often attracts sentimental approval but little status, money or political power. Female-headed households are regularly the poorest in most communities; and the sudden post-natal plunge into invisibility and powerlessness that millions of women experience after childbirth drops many women into clinical depression. In *Sex and Destiny*, Germaine Greer describes how society is organized so as to ignore the mother-and-child dyad: 'They [children] cannot open doors or windows, cannot see on top of counters, are stifled and trampled in crowds, hushed when they speak or cry before strangers, apologised for by harrassed mothers condemned to share their ostracised condition.' Even professional people (of either sex) who care for children often find themselves badly paid and readily maligned. Social workers in New York are sometimes paid less than car park attendants.

Not everyone sees children as valuable human beings. Some adults see them only as toys or leisure pursuits belonging to their parents. As one man put it recently, 'If I decided to go on holiday, I wouldn't expect anyone else to pay or it. If a woman decides to have a baby, why should I pay up?'

But there exists also a growing counter-perception, that children are the seeds of life belonging to all humanity. They are the future – and the best of our present. And some communities do support children and their parents well. In Sweden, for instance, both fathers and mothers are allowed special sick leave when their children are ill: parents don't need to save up their own sick leave for times like this.

Now that the ethos is changing, and children are increasingly seen as a social priority for everyone rather than as a private hobby for parents, the people who have traditionally safe-guarded the rights of children have been joined by people with a higher public profile: lawyers, for instance, and trade union leaders, business people, film-makers, academic researchers, actors, writers, health professionals, religious leaders, and – crucially – government ministers: the sort of people who are in a position to implement the Convention on the Rights of the Child.

Signing the Convention is only a beginning. It has to be implemented, and there are difficulties. Can poor countries afford the Convention? Richer countries already have laws that provide children with more rights than required by the Convention in some areas – most Western countries, for instance, offer more than the universal primary education for which the Convention calls. It is little trouble for

In the West, crèches and nurseries for the children of working parents are now more widely available.

these countries to comply with the Convention's educational requirements but for the government of India, for example, to provide primary education for all its millions of scattered and often destitute children is to undertake a massive task.

Not only do richer countries often have large incomes and small populations, but also a smaller proportion of children compared with the proportion of adults: perhaps only a fifth of their population will consist of children, though children may make up a third or half the total number of people in a poor country. Isn't there a danger that the Convention will be irrelevant in richer countries, and too expensive in poorer ones?

One of the advantages of the Convention being an international document is that governments can ask each other for help in putting children first: they don't need to act alone. The task of looking after children properly can become an opportunity for widening a sense of social responsibility. The situation can be compared to the provision of child care for working parents, which can be envisioned solely as a problem each individual family has to solve by itself – or can be re-visioned as an opportunity for the whole community to consider how children of working parents could be looked after. The community may decide to vary its working patterns, by introducing flexitime or workplace crèches, or paid maternity and paternity leave; or it may even challenge the glorification of 'heroic' workaholism, arguing that it wrecks family life.

In the same way, the child care problems of a nation can provide an opportunity for the international community to question the world's working rules. The old rules of the global marketplace, the long-standing patterns of inequality in trade, aid and debt repayments – these are finally beginning to be challenged in the light of their repercussions on the welfare of children. Is the world's money to be spent on children after buying two-and-a-half thousand million dollars' worth of armaments every day – or are children to be cared for as a priority? Can any country wait 'to be able to afford' good care for children? In the much-quoted paraphrase of the words of the Chilean poet Gabriela Mistral:

Many things can wait. Children cannot. Right now their hip bones are being formed, their blood is being made, their senses are being developed. To them we cannot say tomorrow. THEIR NAME IS TODAY.

RIGHTS AND RESPONSIBILITIES

To give children rights is to do more than to protect children better. It is also to recognize that children have much to offer. Children who have to survive without adult care often show how competent and cooperative they can be. In Chile a group of totally abandoned children under a bridge survived entirely by stealing from the market. Shopping lists were drawn up every day ('We need bread, potatoes, fruit . . .') and tasks distributed. The oldest children went out to 'work' while the middle ones cared for the youngest.

Daniel Defoe, back in 1724, reckoned a child could fend for himself from the age of four or five. Of course we may not want children to spend their lives trying to survive like this: we may prefer children to spend their childhood otherwise, developing and demonstrating their very real potential in ways other than through survival skills. But we must not fall into the trap of thinking that children have to be treated as helpless objects of concern.

To be merely protective towards a child is to dominate him, to smother the development of his own potential. A child who is never allowed to fall over will not learn how to walk; a child who is protected from making any mistake will not learn how to make a decision. The parent who wraps a child in cottonwool – like the mother who refers to her 14-year-old daughter in public as 'my little baby girl' – is disempowering the child as surely as the neglectful parent. Is the over-protective parent 'accidentally' slipping a little of the cottonwool into the daughter's mouth to gag her? Perhaps, like

A child is not just an object of care. A child is a human being with a voice worth listening to.

Carmen (the street child at the children's conference), she might otherwise say what her mother would not like to hear. A good, empowering relationship between adult and child must be a two-way dialogue.

One of the boys who arrived at the street children's conference in Brazil had this to say: 'The generation that sets us the example, brings us up, teaches us, is also the first to criticize us. I came here to give my opinion, to express what I need: warmth, respect, shelter, school and food.' The order in which he placed his needs was worth noting: an adult might have placed food first, but the child gave higher priority to respect.

The Convention does not ask adults to care for children as passive objects. It states clearly in its opening pages that the child has a right to express an opinion and to have that opinion taken into account in any matter affecting the child – and, conversely, that children have the right to be protected from interference with their privacy and their honour. No longer can an adult who falls under the jurisdiction of the Convention assume the right to open a child's letter and read it without consent, nor to attack a child's reputation at whim.

Of course it is true that children are vulnerable. But to say this is not, after all, to say much: adults are vulnerable too, and often the adults who are most sensitive and wise are those who are willing to be most vulnerable. To be vulnerable is to be human – and to want to develop one's powers, one's strengths and talents, and to express them in the service of the community, is also to be human. To develop both sides of human nature – the vulnerable and the powerful, the innocent and the knowing, the yielding and the resilient, the receptive and the expressive – and to explore how best to temper the one with the other, is to learn to be more fully human, whether one is an adult or a child.

An adult acting with responsibility in relation to children means an adult acting with 'response-ability': such an adult is 'able to respond' to each child without the need to distance the child by turning away in pain or by projecting onto him more vulnerability or more power than he actually has. Children's rights are, ultimately, about adults *seeing* children, in their varying combinations of vulnerability and strength, as unique human beings.

There is a widely held adult fear that children will rampage out of control if adults aren't around to corral them and keep them civilized. William Golding, in his novel *Lord of the Flies*, told the story of a group of children shipwrecked on an adult-less island who reverted to savagery and bloodthirsty war – apparently as a metaphor to symbolize the atavistic aspect of human beings that could break out if civilization loosens its grip. But is this metaphor fair on children?

Susanna Agnelli in *Street Children* tells the true story of a group of six boys who had been out fishing near Tonga in 1977 and were washed ashore on an uninhabited island after a storm. They made a promise to each other: that as long as they were on the island they would never quarrel, that they would always go about in pairs, and that two of them would keep guard, day and night. When they were rescued, 15 months later, they had not broken their promise.

2

RICH WORLD RUNAWAYS

I've wasted my childhood on being a man. I was too busy trying to get my life together, trying to locate my parents, trying to put food in my mouth . . . My childhood was stolen from me.

Frank

Frank lives in New York City, on the street. He has lived there since he was 13.

That's how old he was when he was sent away from the Bronx to summer camp – to find, on his return, that his mother and step-father had gathered up their belongings and moved. 'My parents had gone,' he says, recalling his bewilderment. 'I didn't understand what had happened or why . . . until a neighbour called me in and explained that my parents had left.' They left no address where Frank could find them. Their disappearance was no accident: they had planned to move while he was away so that they could 'lose' him.

Frank has worked out a set of reasons to make sense of their rejection. 'I love my mother very much, and my father, but apparently they don't think too highly of me . . . There was some conflict about a newborn baby that was brought into the house; he came out retarded, and they blamed it on me.' This baby that Frank speaks of so distantly, as 'the baby that was brought into the house', is his half-brother – taken away by his mother and step-father when they left Frank behind.

'THE DAMNABLE MASK OF KINDNESS'

Frank was left to find his biological father for shelter. 'My real father is a cocaine fiend. Living with him was no use. He didn't want me there – he was renting out all the rooms.' Frank knows his father's 'reason' is an excuse; he doesn't bother to pretend otherwise. The hurt of this second rejection is written all over his face.

It is clear to him that his father was being as devious about his parental irresponsibility as his mother and step-father had been. 'He shipped me off, told me to go and get a hotel room for a week and that he'd pay at the end of the week. I tried to get the hotel room – and I got laughed at. Because you know you can't get a hotel unless you have the money up front.

'So I went to my father and I told him. And he told me: Besides that he can't help me. If I could get a hotel room, he'd pay at the end of the week – knowing that I can't get a hotel room unless I pay up front.' The victim of this kind of double-bind is trapped: if he accepts the lie, he does so knowing he is being played for a fool; to keep his self-respect he must throw the offer back in the liar's face. Is a 13-year-old supposed to call his 'cocaine-fiend' father a liar?

The people at the hotel laughed at Frank; he knows his father is laughing at him too. To his unwantedness is added humiliation. Herman Hesse wrote feelingly in *A Child's Heart* of a similar experience, of 'some superior deception, such as the grownups and the powerful always contrived, shaming me after all, not taking me seriously, humiliating me under the damnable mask of kindness'. There is no firm ground for a child in this situation to stand on. Parents are supposed to provide security for their children, a safe base from which to explore the unknown world. Parents like Frank's provide a foundation of rejection and duplicity.

It is estimated that 10–20,000 children like Frank live on the streets in New York City. Another 200,000 live rough in California. Estimates vary from half a million homeless children in the United States as a whole to two million. And although most of them tend to be called 'runaways', a large proportion are really 'throwaways' like Frank, abandoned by their families. They have been thrown out of the family circle, scapegoated for family troubles when their presence becomes inconvenient for their parents.

A divorced man, for example, threw out his daughter when his secretary moved in. Journalist Dotson Rader talked to the child who was sitting on the hood of a car:

She said that she was waiting for her boyfriend. Her name was Anabel and she was thirteen. She had short blond hair. The left side was dyed purple. She wore tight jeans, a turtleneck and red boots, and she held a small stuffed doll. Large chandelier earrings dangled from pierced ears. She looked like a child playacting in her mother's clothes.

'My parents got divorced when I was ten,' she told me. 'My father got a new girlfriend. She was his secretary. She moved in with us and we didn't get along. So Dad said it was either Adele or me. We couldn't both stay so he said I had to get out. It hurt me so much. I came down here, where I met Donny.' Anabel spoke in a high, childish voice which she had difficulty controlling. 'Last month I called my Dad and asked if I could come home. He said no, I was too big to live with him now. So I have to stay here.'

What about her mother?

'She says I belong with my Dad,' Anabel said. 'She doesn't want me. So I live in an abandoned house with Donny and some little kids . . . I like to walk around a lot. I see pretty houses and pretend I live there. I want to go home. But I don't have one any more.'

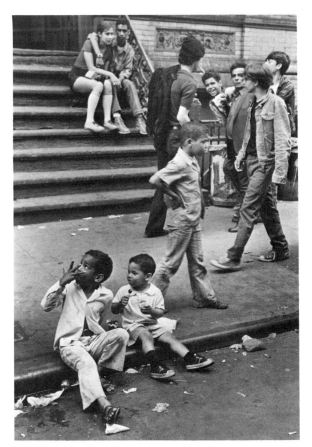

Mean streets: homeless children are often throwaways, not runaways.

'All children have the right to survival, protection and development' –
Convention on the Rights of the Child

'A State should always act in the best interests of the child.'

'The family is the fundamental group of society and the natural environment for the growth of the child.'

The right to a home: children who live on the streets of Bogota, Columbia.

A shanty town on the outskirts of New Delhi, India's modern capital.

The right to health: AIDS babies in New York.

Zambia: a makeshift but effective incubator.

The right to protection from drugs: glue sniffing in Britain.

The right to protection from violence and war: child soldier in Afghanistan.

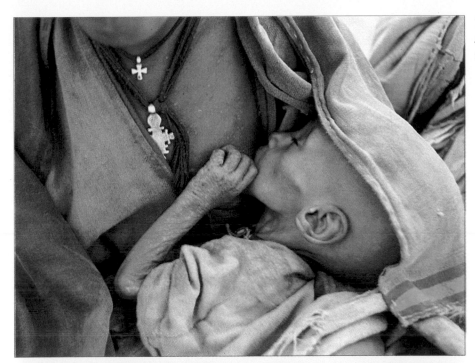

The right to survival: famine victim in Ethiopia.

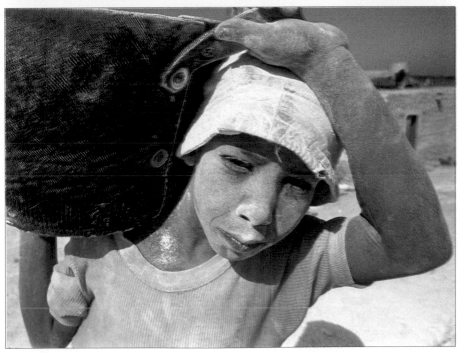

The right to protection from exploitation: child labourer in Egypt.

The right to protection from sexual exploitation: teenage bar-girl in Thailand.

The right of the disabled child to special care and facilities.

The right to education: the best investment a country can make.

The conventional face of New York: Manhattan by night.

The side the world does not see: run-down tenements in West Harlem.

Home for Frank, abandoned by his parents at the age of thirteen, is the top-security wing of a drug rehabilitation centre.

A *handful of 'crack':
a highly-addictive
cocaine-based drug
that is readily
available on the
streets of New York.*

*Mean streets:
children grow up in
a dangerous
environment.*

Abandoned by his parents at the age of 13, home for Frank is now a top security detention centre in the Bronx.

Frank describes other children he has met 'whose parents come from another state, leave them here and then go back; children are being dumped off here that don't even belong in this state'. Says Jed Emerson, director of the Larkin Street Youth Center in San Francisco, 'In 68 per cent of our calls to parents of children who would consider going home the response is, "You keep the kid".'

BREAKING FAMILY TIES

Nevertheless, abandoned children like Frank and Anabel get little sympathy from the public. A frequent response of adults to street children has been the wish to deny their existence: not to think about how they manage to survive, or why they came to be on the street, or what will become of them. Some

adults simply do not 'see' these children. A senior television executive was recently heard to comment at a media conference about world problems: 'Thank heavens we are no longer faced with issues as stark as Dickens.' But Dickens would easily have recognized the children sleeping rough in London or in Lima.

The unpalatable fact is that millions of children in the world live rough on the streets, and not only in poor countries. Poverty cannot explain away the presence of homeless children: many desperately poor families in the developing world do not let their children end up alone on the streets, as hundreds of thousands of children from families in rich countries do. Contrary to popular assumption, the vast majority of the children that are visible on Third World city streets are not abandoned by their families. Sometimes, as in India, the whole family lives on the street: one of the most poignant sights I have seen was of a pavement home. A semi-circle of broken bricks outlined the perimeter, and the space it enclosed was as lovingly tended as any surburban house. Elsewhere, as in Peru, the whole family may spend the day together on the street – selling fruit, perhaps, at a roadside stall. If the parents leave home very early to find the best fruit, an older child may get the younger ones up later, and take them to join their parents at the stall, before leaving for school. After school, this child, too, may join the family group, for a sociable afternoon and evening on the street. For all we know, despite their poverty, these children may be more contented than affluent children whose parents are out all day at plush offices where children are unwelcome.

Only a small minority of the children we see on the streets in poor countries have cut their ties with their families. The dynamics that split families apart in these countries are rarely examined. The assumption that poverty, simply, is the cause isn't helpful: since poverty seems to be too big a problem to tackle, the problem then tends to be shelved, leaving the complex causes of family breakdown unexamined, and the appropriate preventative measures unexplored. One known trigger for children running away is the violence they suffer at the hands of fathers or step-fathers and although the stress of poverty may intensify the possibility of adult male violence against children, such violence clearly has deeper roots.

In the rich world, too, the dynamics of family breakdown are only partly understood. Poverty is certainly not the only issue among the US runaways – the children come from every social background. But family violence, again, seems to be a major factor. According to Ann Donahue, programme director at Covenant House (an emergency shelter in New York for teenage runaways), about 50 per cent of the children who find their way there 'have been physically or sexually abused at home'. Child abuse is widespread. In the United States three children die of abuse at the hands of their parents or guardians every day. In Britain, David Pithers of the National Children's Homes estimates that 70 per cent of child sexual abuse takes place within the family. Another survey suggests that, although the child sexual abusers are not always relatives, they are usually known to the children: only 11 per cent of child sexual abusers were total strangers.

THE DANGEROUS NEST

But society often prefers to deny the dangers within families to children: it is more comforting to think of the family as a safe nest and of most abusers as dangerous strangers who invade the purity of the family if the door is left unlocked. Abusive parents are assumed to be rare and incurable psychopaths. 'Fury as sex monster is freed' screamed the headlines on the front page of Britain's *Daily Mirror* (November 1988) about an abusive step-father – and on its second page another child abuse story bellowed almost as loudly: 'Freed . . . sex slaves who killed evil father'.

To recognize that abusers are ordinary parents in ordinary families is frightening for many people.

The image of the family as a safe nest can be misleading.

The truth is denied and, wherever possible, a scapegoat found outside the family. The events in Cleveland in 1987, where as many as 165 children in one locality were diagnosed by two doctors as being sexually abused, rocked Britain because it blew the myth of the dangerous stranger. The children had to have been assaulted by their fathers or step-fathers – or else the doctors had to be wrong. The force of the public's wish to scapegoat the doctors and to believe the suspected men innocent showed how strenuously people want to deny how dangerous for children families can be. They want to go on believing that fathers will use their power over children to protect them; they don't want to see that that power can be – and often is – misused, especially when there is no counter-power to challenge it. In abusive families, fathers often have power not only over the children but over the mother. Danya Glaser, consultant psychiatrist at Guy's Hospital in London, emphasizes the conventionality of most abusive families, which tend to have a 'rigid adherence to an almost stereotypical patriarchal structure' and 'very traditional sex roles' with few mothers working outside the home and male superiority unquestioned, 'women being treated as having no real rights of their own'.

Writer Beatrix Campbell has drawn a thought-provoking comparison between the public reaction to a sexual abuse case in Britain and another in the United States. In the British case, the family discovered that their small daughter had been sexually assaulted by their lodger, whereupon the father and the brother held him down while the mother poured boiling water over his genitals. When the mother was sentenced for injuring the lodger, there was a public outcry on her behalf and she was freed. In the US case the mother believed that her ex-husband had been sexually abusing their daughter, so she hid the child safely out of his reach. This mother was gaoled for kidnapping her child and there is no public outcry. Campbell sees the calm, rationally planned sacrifice of the American mother, who accepts her imprisonment as a necessary price to pay for her daughter's safety, as unappealing to a public that sympathizes with the violent gut-reaction of the British mother. But there seems to me to be also another, very simple difference. The British family had ganged together to punish the cuckoo in the nest: the American mother was not confronting an intruder but the child's own father; she was challenging the myth about the goodwill of the patriarch in the supposed sanctuary of the family.

The impulse to reject physical or sexual child abusers within the family as rare aberrants helps no one. It makes it harder to recognize the abuse of children in ordinary families and therefore to give them protection – and makes it harder for adults who are willing to admit they have a problem to get help. A spokesman for the UK's National Society for the Prevention of Cruelty to Children commented with relief in early 1989 that more parents were asking directly for help now. But in many, probably most, families, abused children have to find their own routes to survival: leaving home may seem to some the only way to keep their sanity or their lives intact, for the lack of recognition of a child's rights means that children often have little domestic

power. And the double-devaluation of a girl's power puts girls even more at risk than boys, at least in the case of sexual abuse. Three-quarters of incestuous relationships are reckoned to take place between fathers and daughters, the other quarter divided up in the main between fathers and sons, mothers and sons, or brothers and sisters.

Physical and sexual abuse are two of three main categories that experts tend to use to classify child abuse: neglect is the third, and it can come in many forms. Frank's abandonment comes under this category: his physical, mental and emotional care were all neglected the moment his parents moved house and left him behind. Other children, who still live at home, are 'abandoned' in a more subtle and chilling way. Their parents present a cold, permanent refusal to make any humane contact with them, refusing to look the child in the eye or even to call him by name – 'Hey, you' or 'Freak' may be the nearest he gets to a named identity. He may never be affirmed for anything he does or says, only ignored or criticized, until he retreats into a frozen watchfulness, too frightened to initiate a move in case it is the wrong one.

Families that seriously abuse children can be especially catastrophic because society relies on families to act as the child's main bulwark against exploitation. There is a pervasive assumption that the ties of love within a family will mean that all its members will work hard to look after one another. But the ties of love can become deeply confused with the bonds of power, as in this case reported in Britain's *Guardian* newspaper of a 14-year-old girl:

Her father had been having sexual intercourse with her for a year. Previous to that he had manipulated her sexually since the death of her mother six years previously. When she complained of the pain of intercourse, he burned her with matches – to show what real pain was about . . . She was petrified and the last thing she wanted was for her father to go to prison.

The doctor said: 'It's fully understandable that she wants to protect her father. Whatever we think of him, in her eyes he is her provider, and also her lover.'

The child who has been betrayed by her socially designated protector is a child doubly betrayed. When she is hurt, to whom can she turn?

'Runaways are not away from home because it is glamorous,' says Greg Day of Larkin Street. 'These young people are fleeing untenable situations at home.' And the 'untenable situations' that cause them to leave are family dynamics that are profoundly damaging to children, not fits of pique. As Trudee Able-Petersen, ex-prostitute and now street worker, puts it drily, 'It's not because their parents wouldn't let them paint their bedroom black.' Thus, any serious initiatives to counter the problem of children on the street must begin with preventative work within families, to prevent children being abused, or re-abused, in the home. Any other answer, as a teenager once described it to me, is like sending an ambulance to the bottom of a cliff.

OF PIMPS AND PROSTITUTES

The average age for runaway or throwaway children in the United States is 15. Seventy per cent are white, and they come from every social class. Many who escape abuse at home by jumping on to buses that take them to big cities do not realize that the friendly stranger who takes pity on them at the bus terminal, kindly offers them a cup of coffee and takes them home, may be a pimp lying in wait for a

The red light district of New York's 42nd Street, where children are trapped into buying drugs and selling sex.

vulnerable child. The child clings to the pimp as a new protector, becoming more and more emotionally loyal to him – until eventually she consents to prostitute herself for him.

In *The Sexual Exploitation of Children*, Judith Ennew writes that: 'This pattern shows little variation, whether it takes place among runaway girls arriving from the countryside in London, Paris, New York or Mexico City. Once involved in prostitution, the girl can extricate herself only at the risk of losing the spurious stability she has found.' She quotes a Minnesota police officer who made a cogent analysis of the relationship:

The pimp–whore relationship is a very precise one, with rigorously defined and mutually accepted conventions. The primary one – a fundamental part of the game – is that she denies even to herself that he cheats her; and at the same time, she never cheats him. If she does, he punishes her, and in this morbid and pathological relationship she expects and even provokes the punishment . . . this dishonesty . . . is not just part of, it *is* the relationship. It is an emotional corruption which the young girls find almost impossible to erase or reverse, even if they manage to break away from the life.

So the relationship is psychologically (and often physically) a form of sado-masochistic bullying, with the stronger partner always taking and the vulnerable one giving away her sense of worth. Each turn of the cycle 'proves' again to the child her deep-seated belief, established at home, that she is guilty and needs to be punished; that it is therefore fitting when the pimp punishes her; that she is not entitled to love and care. She gives away her belief in her right to be respected as an autonomous human being.

It is understandable enough that the girls or boys – abused or rejected by their families – should have a poor self-image. By why can't they also see that the pimp's behaviour is less than good? In psychological terms, the child is 'projecting' on to the man all her own good qualities, as if on to a screen. When she looks at him she sees not the real man

who is cruel and exploitative, but instead a person reflecting back qualities like devotion and loyalty: the qualities that actually belong to her. If she wants access to these qualities, it seems to her that she must stay with him, not realizing that these good qualities are her own; on the contrary she feels lacking in these very ways. In her imagined inadequacy she clings to him, grateful for his kindness in putting up with her.

The destructive relationship between the pimp and the child-whore is clearly a reprise of the process that began at home when the child's right to her sexuality was consumed instead of protected by her family. Rather than developing the child's sense of autonomy which enables her to feel entitled to her rights, the abusive parent uses the child exploitatively, disabling her with fear, guilt and shame until she imagines herself to be unworthy of having rights. The process provides an example of why it is important that children's rights are socially acknowledged as belonging to children independently of their parents. There is no guarantee that a parent will not abuse his position of domestic power over a child. A child's innate sense of her right to say 'no' to demands by an invasive and manipulative adult can often be tissue-thin: she needs all the support she can get.

BLAMING THE VICTIM

But if children chased from abusive homes into prostitution shouldn't be blamed for trying to survive, neither should the pimps (who are often teenagers themselves) take all of the blame. They didn't invent the child sex market, although they are its brokers. As Able-Petersen's autobiographical *Children of the Evening* shows, they wouldn't be in business if they didn't have regular customers eager for exploitative sex: so many customers, in fact, that thousands of children are kept busy 'turning tricks' several times a night in seedy hotel rooms – when they are not dancing in sex shows, or listening

Trudee Able-Petersen, once a prostitute herself, now works with child prostitutes in Manhattan.

to masturbating men 'talking dirty' to them through the holes in peep show booths that stink of stale semen, sweat and disinfectant.

But however much parental abuse has driven the children away from home, and adult customers keep child prostitution a thriving business, it is the child that tends to be looked at with suspicion as a 'bad kid'. Greg Day says: 'Throwaways have been abused and discarded, and the knee-jerk reaction of society is to consider it a police problem instead of a social problem.'

An otherwise sensitive article in the *Christian Science Monitor* compares the runaways in the rich world unfavourably with Filipino street children, who are described approvingly as 'fighters'. The comment reflects the popular prejudice against the rich world's runaways as self-indulgent romantics. But the serious runaways (those who don't return home within 48 hours) have to be fighters too to stay alive. It doesn't make any difference how rich your parents are: if you've been forced into the street, your empty pockets qualify you quickly as an honorary member of the poor world.

Trudee Able-Petersen is unequivocal: 'We're using the children as a scapegoat when in fact the children are the victims of adults. They are victims of families,

they are victims of systems, and they are certainly the victims of the consumers of child sex.' Not only teenagers but even very young children are scapegoated for adult sexual irresponsibility.

In a court case a few years ago, a man who raped his girlfriend's five-year-old daughter was let off by the judge – on the ground that the child had been provocative. (She had bounced on to the bed where the man was taking a nap.) First the rapist and next the judge preferred to scapegoat a five-year-old girl for her supposedly uncontrolled sexual appetites rather than insist on an adult male taking responsibility for his.

When the world outside the family turns out to be no safer than life inside it, a few children find their way to emergency shelters for homeless adolescents, like New York's Covenant House founded by Father Bruce Ritter. Ritter places the blame for the condition of the street children on every adult who participates in the chain of degradation:

Everybody who watches a hardcore porno film has to know they are part of the problem. If you snort cocaine, you are part of that chain, and you cannot walk away from it. . . . You're part of that chain of corruption and violence and profit to organized crime, and you cannot walk away from it. We live in a sex-for-sale society that shows kids it's okay to become sexual objects; it's okay to become the merchandise in the sex industry – of which we are the patrons.

It is naïve to imagine that only a small and sleazy minority of adults have ever watched pornography or taken drugs: respectable adults are part of Ritter's 'chain of corruption'. So the street child should not be blamed as a source of society's sexual ills but seen to be one of its symptoms: he is a fragile shred of litmus signalling a society where power is misused by those who have much against those who have little. Its hypocrisy is exemplified by the men who move their families away from inner cities to safe suburbs to protect their children from city violence

'Project Enter', a temporary shelter in the middle of Harlem, run by young black social workers. The street children who turn to them for help don't want to leave – but two months is the longest they can stay.

– but cruise back to the city in the evenings to exploit other people's daughters or sons.

Able-Petersen describes Melissa, a 13-year-old girl she once befriended, in her encounter with such a man. Melissa is a runaway who had been abused sexually at home over a long period; when she worked as a child prostitute for a pimp, she was savagely attacked by him, ending up in hospital with vaginal lacerations from broken glass. On this occasion, she was coping on her own: 'Melissa was hungry. She wished she'd held on to some of that five [dollar bill] for another pizza. She strolled over to Ninth Avenue . . . walking very slowly so she'd be visible. Finally she noticed a car that had circled her twice. The blue sedan pulled up beside her.'

After a short bargaining session in which the man knocked down the price he was willing to pay her, Melissa got in the car and dealt with the man's sexual wants – and then he dropped her off hastily to head home for New Jersey. 'He had to hurry, he told Melissa, because his daughter had a part in the eighth-grade play and she would be terribly unhappy if her daddy was late.'

Iain, another street child, had a similar experience. 'I've gone off with a guy that told me I looked like his son,' he said. 'It just freaked me out. How could they be married and have children – and then come and pick up a child like me on the streets and buy him for an hour? I just couldn't ever understand that.' It is hard to understand. How can the same adult speak of children in two such different ways – in one breath as sons or daughters whose feelings must be meticulously protected, and in the next breath as sellers of sex, whose market price has to be knocked down? When the children even look the same, mirror images of one another, how can an adult see one as deserving of every good and the other as deserving of none?

Psychologist Chris Robertson offers a clue. Scapegoats are not always sacrificial goats, he explains, although that is how the word is popularly used. 'There is the good scapegoat and the bad,' he says, and only the bad is sacrificed. We project on to the bad scapegoat the shadowy sides of ourselves that we are ashamed of and prefer to deny, and sacrifice this scapegoat to 'get rid of' what we do not want to face. But we project our idealizations on to the good scapegoat, whom we protect adoringly. The real child before us, in either instance, we fail to see; all we see is one or other of our split-off projections (just as the child-prostitute sees not the real pimp but her own projected qualities). In this way a parent casts his child into an idealized mould: these precious children must be treated with great care, their finer feelings kept inviolable. But as for the child dumped on the street – her feelings can be violated to any degree, for this child is the 'bad' goat, the one who is sacrificed.

HALF IN LOVE WITH EASEFUL DEATH

Frank has been a drug user and a drug pusher, not surprisingly given his father's activities with cocaine. In any case, drugs are the norm on the streets. Bereft of dreams to live their lives by, drugs become the street children's *raison d'être*. 'Getting and selling we lay waste our lives,' William Wordsworth once wrote, and his words are probably more true of the drug-dealing street child than almost anyone else.

A child on the street survives by selling drugs or by selling his body. And if he sells his body, he probably buys drugs: a child who sells himself for a hundred dollars at night may blow it all the next morning on drugs to blunt the horror of the following night. His days and nights revolve in a slow act of suicide. Able-Petersen describes how, in her prostituting days, she used to take mind-blotting drugs to keep her from gagging at the loose skin flapping in her face, as middle-aged customers gasped and sweated over her.

New York has become more violent as addiction to crack – cocaine at its deadliest and most addictive – becomes an epidemic. It has been estimated that there will be more than a million crack addicts in the United States this year. Crack is cocaine baked into crystals with baking powder and ammonia, then smoked. It induces aggression, hyperactivity, breathlessness, and the craving, within moments, for more.

Adults who use drug-soaked child prostitutes are condoning the half-life that these children have to live; some customers ('tricks') even encourage the children's drugged existence by paying them in 'crystal' (drugs) instead of in cash. The teenage 'hookers' say they hate these 'crystal tricks' who make sure they stay hooked. And the question must be asked: who is the hooker here, and who is the hooked?

The drug problem is growing not only in numbers but in complexity. 'Hot rocks' are heroin and cocaine combined; 'champagne' is crack sprinkled in marijuana; 'supercrack' is crack combined with amphetamines. These combinations are creating a new class of users with strong multiple-addictions that are even more perplexing to treat.

Says Frank: 'Today it's hard out there, real hard. There are just so many children being abandoned, abused, involved with drugs, that I don't think the city can handle it no more. I mean, you've got children having children without wanting them; they don't know how to treat them.' If these pregnant teenagers have been addicted to drugs, so will their babies be. Babies are automatically fed drugs while still in the womb if the mother is a drug addict. As crack sweeps across US cities, more and more crack

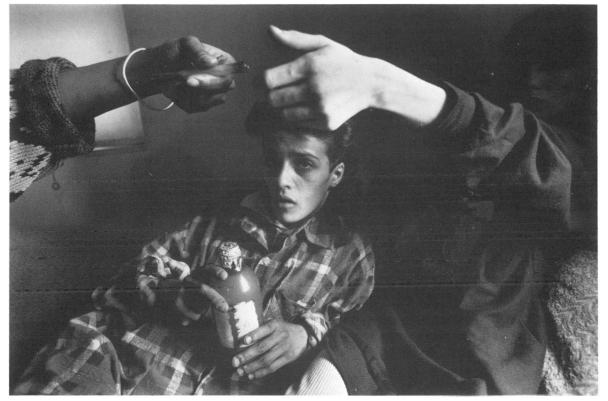

Crack Annie, 17, lives in a crack den run by two girls in Red Hook, Brooklyn, New York. She supports her habit through prostitution.

babies are being born: tiny, underweight babies who constantly shudder and retch, who sweat and tremble or scream helplessly in the pain of withdrawal. If their mothers have been polydrug abusers, the babies must go through a separate withdrawal for each substance to which the mother is addicted. Some are born with missing or deformed limbs. Even in a land short of babies to adopt, not many parents volunteer to adopt a baby like one of these, the saddest babies in America.

'One in twenty adult residents of New York State is involved in some form of serious drug abuse,' says Dr Lorraine Hale, director of Hale House, a home for babies born addicted. Such babies have a

fragile hold on life: usually underweight and often premature, the fleeting mark they leave on life is recorded most visibly in New York's soaring infant mortality figures. If they do survive the early weeks in hospital, who will care for them then? Not the stoned parents spending a hundred dollars a day on drugs. And, according to Dr Hale, until recently infant addiction has been denied as a reality by state authorities: 'Not so long ago even the National Infant Drug Abuse agency had its funding removed because the government claimed there was no such thing as an infant addict.' Denial, by the adults with power and money, is a response that shields them from the pain of recognizing what one generation

Drugs can kill: a teenager is buried in New York City.

does to the next. But such denial protects the powerful at the cost of betraying the powerless.

Edward Barnes reported in Britain's *Sunday Times* newspaper that at the Red Hook housing project in South Brooklyn, New York, 'Dealers with guns and money run the streets: they shoot each other and anyone else who gets in the way.' The source of the drugs and the violence isn't in poverty-stricken Red Hook itself – it slides in from a richer world outside to feed on the misery it finds there:

When David 'Dumar' Ross's unblemished white Lincoln Town Car drives into Red Hook, a potent symbol of power and immunity, the dealers and lookouts crowd around, each hoping to be given an errand to run or a task to be performed for the great man. Dumar, 6ft 4in and 22 stone, is Mr Big in every sense. He dominates the Hook's

drug trade: nobody operates there without his sanction. Those who say they are with Dumar, he says, remain unshot.

In a neighbourhood like this, being the most powerful means being the most violent. Here, once more, is the same sado-masochistic pattern that exists between the pimp and the child-prostitute, or the abusive father and the dependent child, although this time it is underlined with bullets. The weak and vulnerable cling to the protector who is the same person from whom they most need to be protected; the 'benevolent' patriarch, the Mr Big, at the top of the hierarchy who absorbs all the centralized power, protecting those who live by his rules and punishing those who disobey.

If drugs don't kill these children, there is AIDS

through shared needles, or AIDS through sex. Or murder by pimps and drug pushers. Pete Axthelm, who investigated the lives of street children for *Newsweek* magazine, believes that more than 5,000 American teenagers a year are buried in unmarked graves. 'AIDS is not a dominant fear on the streets,' he says. 'Hour to hour, there is enough else to be afraid about.' Death lies in the future – and children on the street can't afford to think that far ahead. You can't plan the future when you have no base to stand on in the present: no emotional security, no financial guarantees, no roof over your head. You can't get state welfare if you don't have a fixed address to give, and it's illegal to get a job if you're under-age. Selling sex and drugs may not look like a route to death but like the only available route to survival.

Some of the children who do let in the awareness of death are past caring. Pete Axthelm heard one say: 'The tricks are sick for picking me up and I'm sick for doing it. . . . You learn to survive. But you also learn not to care if you don't.' About 7,000 teenagers in the United States commit suicide each year, according to *Reflections*, a publication produced by a voluntary agency helping teenagers. 'It is the second highest cause of death among young people aged fifteen to twenty, and its incidence is growing.' And it has been estimated that for every child who commits suicide there are at least 100 others who attempt it.

And who mourns the street children who die, apart from other street children? 'There's no one else to mourn these children,' replies Trudee Able-Petersen, sadly. 'No one else.'

CARING FOR THE FALL-OUT

The difficulties facing the rich world's runaways are at last beginning to be taken more seriously, at least in the United States, although the response is inadequate to the scale of the problem and tends to focus on crisis-care rather than on prevention.

Telephone hotline centres set up for children around the country report as many as a thousand calls a day – each. The Trailways Corporation offered a free ride home to any runaway who wanted one, and between summer 1984 and 1985, they transported more than 4,500 runaways. Emergency shelters like Covenant House and Larkin Street have been springing up around the country: the number of shelters has increased from less than 150 in the mid-1970s to over 500 in the mid-1980s. A Suicide Prevention and Treatment in Runaway Shelters Project was begun in New York in 1986.

New York's The Door is a centre that provides a slightly different kind of shelter for children. 'Every time you step into The Door,' says one child, 'it gives you a natural high.' The Door helps children who have benefited from crisis-intervention when they were in trouble and who are now ready to take the next step; and it has become a model for such centres in other parts of North and Central America. The range of services it offers is impressive: from health care and legal assistance all the way to a 'young people's performing arts company' or weekend hiking trips in the woodlands of upstate New York.

Even the building is designed with imagination and freedom to mirror the new possibilities opening up for its guests: unconventional shapes and perspectives have been used everywhere to encourage change – circular, ellipsoid, hexagonal and free forms which, the organizers hope, will serve as a means of breaking up the stereotyped ways of seeing and feeling that are reinforced by traditional hard-edged cubical rooms. Bright colours and open spaces contrast with the cramped grey spaces that the children usually see. 'Everything about the place invites you to go in, to see what's happening and join in the action,' says another child.

Most important of all, the children here, who have been treated for years as impersonal objects passed from hand to hand, are now offered a counsellor who will stay with a particular child throughout his or her relationship with The Door.

Rap at 'The Door': each child is a special child. Teenagers referred here get a glimpse of what life can offer – and what they can offer back.

At last the child is recognized as a unique individual, cared for as someone special by someone special, not seen just as an object of concern. And these counsellors also attempt to do what adults ideally should do for children: show them that the world can be a beautiful, healthy and fascinating place – and that these children have a part to play in it.

But only a tiny minority of children are helped by organizations like this. Post-crisis, piece-meal, voluntary intervention can never be enough: there must be large-scale, nationally funded preventative action, so that families know where they can turn for reliable help before family problems go out of control. This sort of help is expensive and time-consuming, but the state of New York seems willing to spend money on children in trouble. So why is there still such a problem?

Marcia Lowry is a New Yorker and a lawyer who agrees that millions of dollars are being spent on state care and that there are reasonable laws on the stature books. The problem lies in the way these resources are applied: as blunt instruments too unresponsive to the needs of particular children in particular families. 'The law says that the state should intervene if the child is in imminent danger, and it also says the state should make efforts to keep the child with the family if there is a reasonable way to do that,' she says. 'But the child welfare system is so poorly administered that we remove the children who should stay and leave behind the children who should be removed.' To make matters worse, the state takes the children away without due preparation:

The state tries to place these kids without any information either about the kids or about the places – it just calls people up and says 'Could you take this kid tonight?' There's no management whatever – it's absolute chaos. There's no system, no procedures; the child is moved from place to place, often into highly inappropriate places: little children snatched from their families and put in big buildings with staff who don't know their names.

Can you imagine what it does to a two-year-old to be called 'Hey you', and moved from place to place with no idea of why or where they are going! Just think how frightening it is to be taken out of a familiar environment, even an unpleasant environment, and never have any idea what's going to happen. Over a period of time it totally destroys a child. Eventually you can create a person who has no idea of human relationships, who has no idea of affection. It is no wonder these little kids who were taken away are growing up to be people that we are worried about as threats to society. I think it's amazing that they are not all trying to kill everybody, given what's happened to them.

We have created these kids; we have put them into the terrible shape they are in – and then we look at them and say, 'How damaged they are – how can you expect anybody to do anything reasonable for them?'

She says bluntly:

We have two kinds of abuse. We have the parents or caretakers who abuse children – and then we have the government itself abusing children once it takes custody. The state is the most abusive parent we've got. It's a very serious problem and it's getting worse.

Whether or not to remove a child from an abusive family is a painfully tricky decision to make under the best circumstances. But the circumstances are far from good when they are made by undertrained, overloaded social workers, too often ignorant of the community language or culture in which they work. José Nazario of Mobilization for Youth says, 'It is easy to blame the social workers. They make easy scapegoats.' But there simply aren't enough experienced social workers in the United States to cope. There are nearly half a million children already in care – and some two-and-a-half million new cases of child abuse are reported every year. There aren't enough 'ground troops' employed by the welfare service to provide the massive response required, when hotlines flood in thousands of calls each day. Nor is it a tempting profession to join, with high stress and low pay.

In Britain, too, there is a shortage of adults ready to respond to abused children. Dr Alan Gilmour, director of the NSPCC, writes in *Innocent Victims* that:

The NSPCC policy for its staff is that any alleged incident of child abuse should be investigated urgently, within a maximum of 12 hours. *A Child in Mind* [the public inquiry report after the death of Kimberley Carlile] suggests that the time limit for social services . . . should be 24 hours. But if there are no social workers available, what can be done? . . .

Conscientious workers can be confronted by an unacceptable dilemma: faced with an impossible workload, too few colleagues and inadequate support or training, do you work at the pace which you can responsibly manage, ignoring all other cases because you know you cannot cope with them, whatever possible risks are being faced by the children involved? Or do you cut corners, race around as many cases as you can, taking snap decisions which you hope will be right – but aware all the time that you could in your haste be missing vital evidence and taking wrong decisions?

Despite the pressures already weighing on social workers, the government's response has been unhelpful. 'Unfortunately,' writes Dr Gilmour, 'the pruning of expenditure has continued and essential services are being eroded.'

NEW HOMES FOR OLD

In New York City, José Nazario believes there is just as much reported abuse in foster families provided by the state as in other families. And even foster homes run by caring families cannot provide what children really need since fostering is, by definition, temporary. Adoption is permanent, but adoptive parents usually queue up for newborn babies, not for teenagers with emotional and drug problems. Stability is what these children lack above all else. They need parenting by adults who remain lovingly responsive for more than a few months at a time.

Frank is by now an expert on adult rejection. He remembers all too well how he was moved from place to place and how emotionally disruptive it was. He says:

All the places you go to want to take responsibility over you and want to be your parent – and I tell you something, if they were supposed to be my parents, I must have went through thirty parents already, because I have been in so many places! But it's nothing like being with parents because each place will decide to let you go in a matter of a minute . . . They let you go real quick.

Cathy, a much-fostered teenager, sums up her experience of fostering in one bitter line: 'Who's going to give you up next?'

None the less, as someone who has been on the receiving end of state intervention, Frank's feelings about it are not entirely negative. He says in the same breath that 'the city sets you up' and that 'the city helps you'. If it wasn't for the city, he reckons, he might no longer be alive. Frank lives now in the top-security wing of a detention centre – and for the first time in his life he feels safe. At last he is in the care of adults with whom he has a stable relationship; he is on a rehabilitation scheme to help him come off drugs; and he is studying hard, so that he will have qualifications for a job when he is released.

Does Frank's new 'home' in a cell, with prison warders for 'parents', count as success or tragedy, or both? For children with less sympathetic prison officers, there may only be tragedy. The detention centres that some street children find themselves in do nothing to help the children: they serve only to keep the streets clear for respectable citizens who feel inconvenienced by children who beg or hustle to stay alive.

But even the best-run detention centres for children care for family fall-out: they pick up the pieces after the crisis has struck. What about preventative care? Marcia Lowry says:

In theory we have a preventative approach, but we're not bothering to spend the money on prevention, we'll spend it instead on keeping these kids warehoused for ten years until they grow up to go into our adult criminal system – and cost society even more money then . . . New York is spending an enormous amount of money in an incredibly tragic way. We are destroying these children at great public expense.

It seems, then, that there is a willingness to help children in trouble: but that help seems to be offered to families or to street children too often in chaotic haste as problematic objects, rather than as persons who need more subtle, sensitive adult responses.

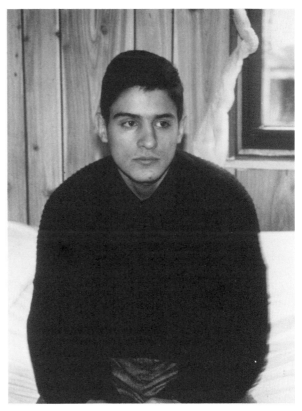

Frank, in detention at sixteen, has a stable relationship with adults at last. He has accepted the chance to study and to come off drugs.

GLIMPSES OF A LOST CHILDHOOD

All this rejection batters the teenager who is still a child under the cool veneer. Frank, now 16 years old, talks with delight in his voice about going to the zoo for the first time on a prison outing. 'I didn't think it would be so nice. There were so many animals! I've wasted my childhood on being a man. I was too busy trying to get my life together, trying to locate my parents, trying to put food in my mouth . . . My childhood was stolen from me.'

Able-Petersen tells a poignant story about a sophisticated young prostitute she got to know. She asked the girl what she would like for her eighteenth birthday: 'It was one of the saddest things – she wanted a colouring book and crayons.' And when she got them, all her friends crowded around, longing to join in. 'When you've been robbed of your childhood by these hard-life experiences,' says Able-Petersen, 'you're not going to be like other children – and yet your needs are those of any child. They say again and again, "I wish I had a family, I wish I could go home, I wish my family was different." I see children returning home again and again to abusive parents, hoping they will have changed . . .'

The ultimate disowning occurs when not only the family but the state gives a child up to death. Joan Ruhnke's job is to review the cases of children convicted of murder. The recurrent theme in many of these children's lives is that they were rescued from parents deemed unfit by society. So didn't society, as the child's new parents, do any better? Says Ruhnke:

Removal from a dangerous home is supposed to offer more to a child: increased opportunities to grow and thrive, to know love and security. Too often these opportunities are warped by their progress through filters of changing caseworkers, laws and placements. The only certainty for a child becomes the one that nothing is sure or lasting.

Not all children in public care become murderers. When one does, however, the failure of the state as parent is as real as that of a natural one. The state that imposes the death penalty in such a case must realize that it is killing its child.

But isn't it illegal in the United States for the state to kill a child? Yes — but the child may be kept incarcerated until he reaches 18; and then the state can put him to death. Says Ruhnke, 'In their killing, the [children] simply reflect life as they know it: a cruel, cold and remorseless experience.' Adults are blaming the child who murders for not respecting the rights of his victim; for being driven only by his own egocentric fear or anger. And yet is that not exactly how the child's parents, first in the form of an abusing family and then in the form of the state, have treated him? As Ruhnke puts it:

When the state, acting *in loco parentis*, fails abysmally and creates an inhuman being, killing that being represents a final denial of guilt and involvement. . . . I do not want to meet these young killers in the street, but my responsibility to them is real. I am part of what made them; I have allowed government to rear them in a way that has led to this dark, intolerable place. Their living presence serves to remind us all of the consequences of social isolation, of ignoring the suffering of others.

3

A STITCH TOO LATE

You don't actually have to like children very much to want them to have the best start in life.

Gopamma, aged eight, looks immaculate. Not a hair is out of place as it is smoothed back and divided into two crisp braids, looped on either side of her face. Red ribbons match the red of her dress. Gopamma looks out from this neat frame: an intelligent, vulnerable and classically beautiful child. We are charmed even before she comes forward to greet us – and then startled.

The perfectly groomed child with the perfect face has dropped down on all fours to walk. The small of her back is raised high in the air as she perches on hands and feet, legs stiffly stretched, head down. It is an undignified posture, awkward and painful, but it is the only way Gopamma can walk.

Walking at all, even like this, is a victory. When Gopamma was two she contracted polio from pollution in the pool of water in her East Indian village. After her illness Gopamma couldn't walk at all. She could move only by folding her legs underneath her like a cross and dragging herself slowly forward with her hands – or slithering on her belly 'like a snake', as her parents describe it, distressed at the recollection.

Of those sad days, Gopamma says, 'I couldn't go to school and I couldn't play.' The other children ignored her or made fun of her – except for one little girl, Nagalakshmi, who has remained her friend. Most of the day, says Gopamma's mother, she would sit by the side of the road with a sad face, looking at the other children playing.

Gopamma's parents were bitter and fearful when their daughter contracted polio. They would look after her, of course, as long as they could – but what about her future? She couldn't fend for herself, and she would be unmarriageable. Relatives would visit the house and exclaim: 'What will you do with this crippled girl? What will become of her?' Altogether the family paid out 5,000 Indian rupees ($320) to doctors to help cure Gopamma's illness despite their poverty. They own only half an acre, which yields 30 bags of rice each year, of which the family needs 25 to eat. The remaining five are worth about Rs 650.

To make ends meet her father hires himself out as a coolie on other people's farms. In the planting and harvesting season, he earns an extra Rs 10–15 a day. The season lasts for 30–90 days, so the family income is increased by a few hundred more rupees. Their annual cash income is Rs 1–2,000 a year, so by the time they had paid Gopamma's medical bills, they were afraid of getting into debt and bonded labour. Gopamma's father was feeling the weight of family responsibilities 'like a bullock pulling a cart'.

33

Gopamma and her family: only the youngest child has been immunized.

Gopamma had her first corrective surgery at Arthwick Samata Mandal's hospital. Arthwick Samata Mandal (ASM) is a local organization, founded on Gandhian principles, which built a hospital to help the poor with financial help from the Save the Children Fund. When ASM workers trawled the villages for children to help, they found Gopamma. She has had two operations so far; after a third, she should be able to walk upright.

And Gopamma's parents were informed about the vaccine that could have prevented polio for a minute fraction of the cost of Gopamma's expensive and painful curative operations. Gopamma's mother has now had her youngest child immunized against polio, although she had to pay a private

doctor to give them the vaccine: 'a stitch in time saves nine' is no cliché for them.

Gopamma is a survivor. She goes to school already, despite the awkwardness of walking on hands and feet. The local government school is about three-quarters of a mile away; her elder brother Malleswara, aged ten, carries her to school on his back. We saw her in the schoolhouse, vigorously chanting a rhyme along with her classmates, only occasionally losing the thread in confusion. She wants to catch up on the lost years of education; she wants to become a teacher who tells other people about the importance of polio immunization. Given her determination and her supportive family, she probably will.

*After years of being hidden away at home,
Gopamma now goes to school.*

The tragedy lies in the irreplaceable years of her childhood, stolen by a disease that could have been prevented for a few cents' worth of vaccine. Every year nearly 200,000 children in India add to the list of polio's living victims – though if Gopamma had been born in Europe or North America she would almost certainly have escaped the disease. Paralytic polio has virtually disappeared in the industrialized countries of the North, although as recently as the 1950s there were tens of thousands of cases. What brought about such an improvement in the North – and why not in the South?

IMMUNIZING ALL THE CHILDREN IN INDIA

The discovery of a cheap and simple vaccine was the key to the conquest of polio in the North. All the authorities had to do was to pour it (metaphorically speaking) down the health channels that reached out to every family – and the job was done. Even if a few children were missed, the disease would not strike: as long as a critical mass of around 90 per cent of the population are immune, polio does not spread.

But in the South, such health networks did not exist. They had to be set up, nearly from scratch. Huge numbers of medical workers and administrators had to be trained; expensive equipment and clinics had to be found; and a population had to be educated to consume this strange new medication.

Ethically, though, it was a task that could not be ignored. Every year, a quarter of a million children around the planet were being crippled by polio and a further 23,000 children dying. A world which, for the first time in history, knew how to save these children from polio at the cost of a few cents could not morally turn its back on the job. But the practical problems remained.

India had nearly half the world's destitute children. Their families lived in villages and slums scattered across a vast subcontinent – illiterate, speaking hundreds of different languages and dialects, unorganized by public authorities. How could they be reached? Could India afford to build a network for health care, monumental in size and complexity? The counter-argument was that India couldn't afford not to build such an infrastructure. She certainly couldn't afford expensive treatment to

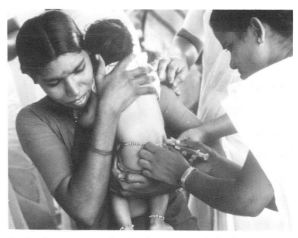

*India has now embarked on one of the largest
immunization programmes in the world.*

35

cure children like Gopamma after they had caught a disease. Prevention, however expensive to set up, had to be cheaper than cure. And the health networks would be useful for immunizing children against not just one or two but all six vaccine-preventable diseases – diphtheria, whooping cough, tetanus, measles, polio and TB.

These six diseases claimed the lives of a million children each year in India alone. The health network could also be used to give anti-tetanus vaccine to babies still in the womb, by injecting their mothers.

So the government of India threw itself into immunizing the nation's children. In 1978, a programme of immunization was initiated in all of India's 420 districts but it reached less than a third of the population. Seven years later, in 1985, Prime Minister Rajiv Gandhi gave the programme a higher profile by committing the nation to universal immunization 'as a living memorial' to his recently assassinated mother, Indira Gandhi.

The challenge of the new plan was to reach 100 per cent coverage in pregnant women and at least 85 per cent coverage in infants by 1990. It meant that, over a five-year period, more than 90 million pregnant women and 83 million infants needed to be immunized. According to the 1988 State of the World's Children Report, 4,800 doctors, 72,000 paramedics and 30,000 other community workers were trained in 1986. As a result, in the 92 districts where the programme was launched that year, immunization coverage roughly doubled (and for measles quadrupled). The following year, the programme moved on to another 90 districts, while maintaining the new level of immunization in the original 92.

CREATIVE COMMUNICATION

Increasing the supply of personnel and equipment needed for this vast immunization programme was not enough: the demand had to be increased as well. People like Gopamma's parents needed to know what immunization could do for their children so that they would seek it out.

Every conceivable means of communication was used to put out the news about immunization. Apart from the obvious ones like radio, television and newspapers, there were the 'non-news media': MPs, religious leaders, business leaders, community elders, child care workers, sports personalities, people in women's groups and youth organizations – they were all approached and encouraged to spread the word.

India has a thriving tradition of popular cinema: advertisements explaining immunization were shown in more than 12,000 cinemas, to audiences totalling an estimated 100 million people. Schoolteachers seemed a good point of contact since they were involved with children every day: 500,000 primary schoolteachers were taught about infant immunization and printed materials were distributed widely throughout primary schools.

Today's schoolchildren are tomorrow's parents. So the effort made by India to immunize this generation of children was planting the seed for the better health of future generations too. A self-renewing cycle of care was being set in motion.

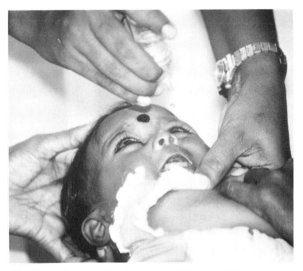

Planting the seed for better health: a child receives a polio vaccine in a drop.

All this social mobilization in India may have another, less tangible but absolutely crucial, effect: people who have been drawn personally into a movement to help children are going to be far more conscious of children's rights to care and protection in general. Groups of people acting on behalf of children's health locally are, knowingly or not, forming the local links of a worldwide health network which includes everyone from heads of state like Rajiv Gandhi of India to 'barefoot doctors' in China.

The child health movement, therefore, has often been called a 'child health revolution', for the movement is concerned not only with saving huge numbers of children but with a switch in the priority which society perceives it must give to children's needs. In the act of saving children's bodies, adult minds are being changed, and their sensitivity to children upgraded. The fundamental right to universal child health care, as enshrined in the Convention on the Rights of the Child, can no longer be written off as the dream of an idealist: it is a revolution already under way.

When President Abdou Diouf was encouraging the Senegalese effort to immunize the nation's children, he caught the spirit of this movement. 'Vaccination is everyone's business!' he said enthusiastically – and the results in Senegal have been breathtaking. In 1985, fewer than 10 per cent of the children had been immunized. Literacy levels are low and few people have access to information through television in Senegal, for it is among the 30 poorest nations in the world. But just two years later, 70 per cent of Senegal's children had been immunized against TB, diphtheria, whooping cough, polio, measles and yellow fever. How was this done?

Parents had been told the immunization story by traditional storytellers beating drums around the villages. Boy Scouts and Girl Guides had gone from home to home spreading the word, and tens of thousands of schoolchildren had informed parents of the time and place of the nearest vaccination session. Youth and sports organizations had held traditional wrestling matches, concerts, and football games where parades of children had marched around wearing T-shirts bearing the slogan 'Vaccination for all children'.

There had been no time nor money to build clinics. So communities had set up temporary immunization posts in mosques, schools, private homes; 'even', says development writer Peter Adamson, 'under a shady tree in the village square'. He describes how trade unions and political parties organized vaccination sessions in offices and factories, and radio was used to reach the illiterate majority, while press and television coverage reached a small but influential minority.

FIVE DOLLARS TO SAVE A LIFE

China provides another success story. It, too, used whatever resources were to hand while its government was building up more sophisticated ones. In 1979, China began producing vaccines at seven regional institutes around the country which distributed the vaccines on an appointed day to provincial health authorities, who rushed them to township distribution points for collection by 'barefoot doctors', who in turn bicycled the vaccine to their villages. Within three years of this 'rush and relay' system the number of measles cases in China fell from a million a year to less than half a million. And, by 1987, according to the State of the World's Children Report, a country with a population of one billion scattered human beings recorded only 439 deaths from measles, diphtheria, whooping cough and polio combined.

The examples of India, Senegal and China show that universal immunization can be achieved even under the most difficult circumstances if the political will is there and the social will is mobilized. These are among the major success stories of our times, it seems. There are ways to move forward, to protect the rights of children.

And the immense cost of not making the effort, in terms of children's suffering, shows how it is essential for immunization to become universally available. UNICEF estimates that just three vaccine-preventable diseases, measles, whooping cough and tetanus, killed

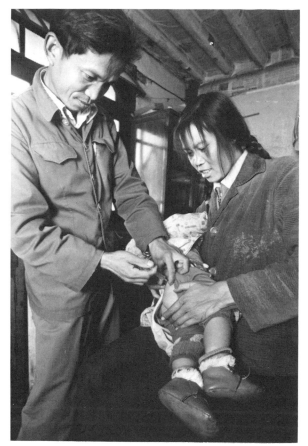

A 'barefoot doctor' brings vaccine to a village in China.

approximately 25 million children during the 1980s: *more than the entire under-five population of the United States and Western Europe.*

Says James Grant, head of UNICEF:

We have the low-cost means to stop that unconscionable carnage and to stop it within the next few years. The lives and limbs of almost all these children could have been spared by a course of vaccine costing approximately five dollars per child. . . . If we do not now use those means, then our pretensions towards civilization and our hopes of human progress will not stand up to any further examination.

In the past fifteen years, international authorities concerned with child health like the World Health Organization (WHO) and UNICEF have been making strenuous efforts to promote universal child immunization. In 1974, fewer than 5 per cent of the children in the developing world were immunized and the WHO's goal of 85 per cent coverage seemed utopian. But immunization levels now average 50 per cent worldwide. Vaccines are estimated to be saving the lives of a million and a half children each year in Africa, Latin America and Asia.

Botswana, Cuba, Egypt, the Gambia, Iraq, Jordan, Oman, Rwanda, Tanzania and Saudi Arabia have already reached, or almost reached, the 85 per cent target. Others like Algeria, Brazil, Kenya, Mexico, Morocco, Pakistan and Turkey, are poised to reach 80–90 per cent coverage by 1990. Startling progress has been made – and demonstrates that more is possible. 'In a little over a decade,' says Dr Ralph Henderson, Director of WHO's immunization programme, with satisfaction, 'a public health revolution has quietly taken place.' And according to UNICEF,

The incidence of polio has been reduced by 25 per cent in the last decade and could be eradicated completely in the next. If progress can be maintained, then the 1980 figure of almost five million child deaths from vaccine-preventable diseases could be reduced to perhaps a quarter of a million or less by the year 2000.

But the revolution has not finished its cycle. Half the world's children may be immunized now – but what about the other half? This half may be harder to reach, not only because of the law of diminishing returns, but because governments are cutting back on public health programmes in the face of international economic pressure. Whether the goal of universal immunization is reached or not depends on us – not on acts of God, or on the weather, but on whether we, as a world, think the task is worth doing. Saving nearly five million lives of children at a cost of just $5 per child: do we think it worth doing? If we think it is, then we have to make our wish clearly known; the immunization of the other 50 per cent of children will not happen automatically.

One of the greatest barriers to universal child health comes not from the poor countries themselves but from the world banking system. The developing countries of the South, as we shall see in the next chapter, are in debt to the rich industrial countries of the North; the money the South would like to spend on child health is being sent to the North as interest payments. The immunization campaign that has done so much for children in the past few years is in danger of faltering. If we want the campaign to continue, we must make our voices heard.

But vaccine-preventable diseases are not the only source of unnecessary child deaths: nine million children each year die of other causes also amenable to simple and dramatic reduction. And in making these reductions too, as we are about to see, the new health networks play a vital role.

CHANNELLING INFORMATION

Diarrhoea is the biggest single killer of the under-fives: between four and five million small children die each year of diarrhoeal diseases. When a child gets a gastric infection, her body sensibly tries to flush out the toxicity; this means she loses a lot of water – and essential salts with it. It is vital for this liquid to be replaced. If not, the child will become dehydrated, and it is this dehydration that leads the child to a lingering and painful death.

In the past, a few dehydrated children were rushed to hospital and saved through the expensive and fiddly business of replacing salt and water intra-venously. Now there is a very simple way to replace the lost fluid at home. Simply dissolve eight teaspoon-fuls of salt and one teaspoonful of sugar in a litre of clean water, and coax the child to drink as much of this fluid as she is losing in diarrhoea. In fact, the hardest part of this treatment is getting a sick child to drink it. Not that the mixture is unpleasant: it

Dehydration caused by diarrhoea kills about five million children a year.

tastes like slightly sweetened tears. The sugar is necessary because the body doesn't absorb plain salty water very well; it tends to pass it out. The dash of sugar acts as a Trojan horse: the body accepts the sugar – and the salt and water ride in with it.

The main stumbling-block to children benefiting from this simple remedy is lack of information. Not enough parents anywhere in the world are aware of the remedy (although it is now being sold in packets to airplane passengers as a cure for jet-lag, which is also related to dehydration). The same child health networks that channelled out the polio vaccine can now channel the knowledge of this life-saving mixture through communities.

Families that use this knowledge could save, by their own efforts, as many as two out of the three children who would have died of diarrhoeal dehydration. Imagine the power of protection this restores to millions of parents, who would otherwise be condemned to stand by helplessly and watch their child waste away in terrible pain, unless they were among the very few who could afford expensive intravenous treatment in hospital.

Today almost a quarter of the children with diarrhoea are being treated with this mixture, or with other similarly constituted fluids like rice water, soups, gruels and fruit juices. WHO estimates that oral rehydration salts (as the remedy is grandly known – or 'ORS' for short) may now be preventing as many as a million deaths a year.

Apart from diarrhoeal dehydration and vaccine-preventable diseases, the biggest killers of small

A Pakistani father gives his child a home-made mixture of sugar, salt and water.

children are respiratory infections, which kill nearly three million under-fives in the developing world. But there are, once again, cheap remedies available for such children. Respiratory infections can now be treated by a mere 50 cents' worth of antibiotics administered by a community health worker.

The next most important means of reducing child deaths, in UNICEF's opinion, is birth-spacing. For the safety of both the mother and the child, the recommended gap between births is two-and-a-half years: otherwise the mother's body has no time to recover before she is pregnant again. Fred Sai, population adviser to the World Bank, has spoken of the 'violence to women and girls' of a lifetime spent in childbirth. By the age of 30, a woman in the poor world has often spent 80 per cent of her adult life either pregnant or breastfeeding. Along the same health networks could be passed essential information about family planning so that families could choose, if they wished, to widen the spaces between births. Births that are 'too many or too close', and births to women who are 'too old or too young' are reckoned to be responsible for up to a quarter of all maternal and infant deaths.

Just these few low-cost interventions – immunization, the use of ORS, cheap antibiotics and birth-spacing – delivered via a new health network, combine to make it possible to save *most of the million children a month that die unnecessarily today.*

The health network set up to service the immunization campaign, as we have seen, places a 'stitch in time that saves nine' every time it immunizes a child, since a preventative vaccination saves so much pain and expense later. A single 'stitch', for Gopamma, in the form of polio vaccine, would have saved her 'nine stitches' of elaborate operations later. And further, having the network in place is in itself a timely stitch. Each time a health message needs to be delivered to the population at large, like the message about the rehydration salts, the channels for reaching local communities will be ready and waiting. Ideally, the channels could work both ways: messages could flow not only from the ministry of health to the people, but also from the people, making their needs and wishes known to health ministries.

Allowing for the time it always takes for health messages to be put into practice, UNICEF's target is a reduction of 50 per cent of child deaths by the year 2000. But a lack of parental information is not the only stumbling-block to reaching this goal. The greatest hindrance to child health lies outside the parents' immediate control.

THE FUNDAMENTAL PROBLEM

Doctors trying to encourage the use of the rehydration salts as a remedy for infant diarrhoea realized that many of the families might not have easy access to clean water; but what they also discovered, heart-breakingly, was that many families were too poor even to have sugar in the house. It brings home the inescapable truth: the underlying cause of most child deaths, whatever the trigger, is a lack of money.

The stark fact is that 97 per cent of child deaths occur in the poor world. Ultimately, the best preventative medicine for child survival would be a just world economic system.

During the past two hundred years or so, historians tell us, in Europe it was not the scientific magic of drugs like penicillin but the everyday reality of money being spent on public drains, and money being distributed more fairly among the population, that caused such a leap in the level of public health. A generally clean, healthy and prosperous environment makes the biggest difference. 'More than half of all illness,' says Peter Adamson, 'is associated with inadequate hygiene. In communities without safe water and sanitation, it is very difficult to prevent contamination of food and water.'

At present, those parents who can least afford to treat their children when they fall sick are also the parents forced to bring their children up in the most

Communities that can least afford to treat sick children are also the communities with least access to clean water and sanitation.

sickness-producing, insanitary environments. The rich choose where they prefer to live: the poor live wherever they may — in shanty towns, beside filthy rivers, on lead-polluted highway verges.

Living in poverty means that children can die suddenly of minor ailments. An elderly Englishwoman who had made friends with a three-year-old child when she was visiting India said to me sadly, 'She didn't come to play with me for a few days, and I heard she had a cold. I waited for her to get well because I thought, of course, that I would see her soon. The next thing I heard, she was dead.'

She is still shocked and puzzled that a misfortune as slight as a cold could have carried off a playful child.

Why are diseases that would only make a child in the North a little poorly lethal among the poor of the South? A well-fed child could shake off a mild cold, eat heartily to replace any lost reserves and bounce back none the worse – thoroughly stocked up with energy to combat the next infection. But an undernourished child may use up all her meagre bodily reserves to fight one mild infection; and then, since there will be no extra food in the house to help her recover and restock her reserves, the next infection that comes along (and where she

lives, infections circulate freely) will find her even more vulnerable. This second infection will eat into essential body energy and tissue, making her more vulnerable still to a third. The child becomes more and more susceptible to infections as she can summon less and less energy to fight them: she is sliding down the vicious spiral of ill-health. When her hold on life is fragile, a common cold can be enough to extinguish her.

'Undernutrition was a contributing cause in perhaps one-third of the fourteen million child deaths in the world last year,' says the State of the World's Children Report. It warns us, therefore, that even the child health successes that have come

Chimbote, Peru: a family visits a child's grave in the cemetery of the poor, where 80 per cent of the graves are those of children.

through the establishment of health networks must be seen as battles won, not war. The wars still to be won are the wars on political and economic injustice.

Tarzie Vittachi, former External Affairs Director at UNICEF, gave me for my own children the packet of ORS he carried around with him in his pocket as a useful medicine. But as he handed it over, he was anxious to emphasize the context of injustice within which child death occurs:

The very real success of ORS should never obscure the injustice that lies at the heart of all this devastation. Answer a simple question: why do children in poor families fall sick and die so much oftener than children in rich families? We can find remedies, we can persuade people to use remedies – but we must never stop asking ourselves why these children are more vulnerable to sickness in the first place.

It's not that their parents love them any less. It's not that they don't work hard to take care of them. *It's because they are poor.* Good food, pure water, drains, sanitation – how are these to be found, to make the environment that the children grow up in safe and wholesome? Individual parents with only enough time and money to survive from day to day can't solve all that by themselves. Economic justice is needed in the community, in the nation, in the world – otherwise the health of children will continue merely to be tinkered with, *after* they fall sick.

They need their health guaranteed from the day they are born – no, from the day they are conceived. And that means the parents of poor children having the same access to basic resources for their children as rich parents. When are we going to do something about that?

Discrimination by wealth begins even before birth. Mothers who are undernourished during pregnancy are more likely to give birth to undernourished babies – and these weak little babies are far more susceptible to illness and death: low-birthweight babies are four to six times more susceptible to physical and mental handicap, and eight to ten times more likely to die in the first year of life. (A 'low-birthweight baby', officially, is one who is born weighing less than 2,500 grammes – about 5.5

pounds; the average English baby boy weighs about 7.5 pounds.)

Twenty-three million low-birthweight babies are born every year – 90 per cent of them in the poor world. What can be done to protect a baby from beginning life with such a handicap? Compensation for these deficiencies after birth is expensive: prevention is cheap. A study of Guatemalan mothers showed that 9 cents' worth of locally grown foodstuffs a day provided them with the extra nutrients they needed during pregnancy.

CARING FOR THE CARE-GIVERS

If babies are to be properly cared for, so must their mothers. The chances of dying of causes related to pregnancy and childbirth are *40 times* greater, on

A mother is 40 times more likely to die in pregnancy or childbirth in the Third World.

43

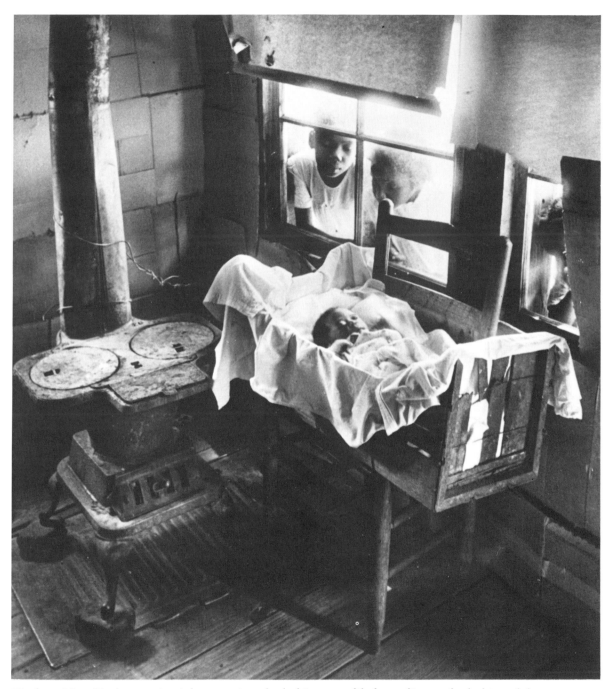

Harlem, New York: even in rich countries, the babies most likely to die are the babies of the poor.

average, for a mother in the poor world than for a mother in the rich world – in some countries as much as 150 times greater. Half a million mothers die in childbirth every year, leaving behind millions of motherless children.

'It is intolerable,' says Dr Attiya Inayatullah, Pakistan's Population Minister, 'that so many women are dying painful, lonely deaths in the process of giving life and we are doing so little to stop it.' And why are we? Dr Halfdan Mahler, former head of WHO, believes the world turns an indifferent eye to the suffering of the disempowered: 'Is it because the majority of these women are poor that they are allowed to suffer this silent carnage?'

Even in rich countries, the babies who are more likely to die are the babies of the poor. If a baby is born into a family kept poor by racial or class discrimination, that baby's chances of survival shrink dramatically. In the United States, the infant death rate was 11 per thousand live births for white babies in 1980 – but 21 per thousand for black babies. In South Africa, the death rate for white babies was 12 per thousand – and for black babies born in the 'Homelands', it was 300.

If a baby is not only poor and black but a girl, her chances of survival dwindle still further. Girl babies are biologically stronger at birth, so at the moment of childbirth, girls' survival rates are often higher than boys'. Nature favours girls: human society favours boys. Discrimination in favour of boys takes over as soon as people know the sex of the child – and before boys reach their fourth birthday, their survival rate has measurably overtaken that of the girls. In Barbados, for instance, at birth and in the first months after birth, for every 100 deaths in boy babies, only 93 girl babies die. But the picture keeps changing. By the age of four, for every 100 boy deaths, there are 200 deaths in girls.

So although we must support actions like immunization or ORS to increase child survival, we need to recognize that there are fundamental problems not addressed by the measure of protection brought about by top-down medical intervention.

Real protection would involve the eradication of social injustice: the inequality that is perpetuated by racism, sexism, and the tolerance of poverty. The truth must never be covered over, even by the success of particular interventions, that children are so vulnerable to illness not only because they are naturally so but because their vulnerability is compounded by man-made problems. Bad politics are more lethal than bad bacteria.

A quarter of the deaths in the world this year will be of children not yet five years old, two-thirds of them still infants –and 97 per cent of them in poor countries. In a rich and bountiful world, why do we let so many children live such brief and painful lives?

And yet, even the poorest mother receives one priceless gift from Nature for her baby.

NATURE'S IMMUNIZER

Without the need for politicians, research biologists or infrastructure, Nature has devised a system of immunizing babies that is so subtle and precise no human scientist could ever match it. This is the natural immunization that comes from breastmilk.

A mother's milk not only feeds babies, as we all know, but it immunizes them. Newly born infants are at risk from the infections swirling around them but an infant can 'borrow' his mother's immunity, by drinking it in with the breastmilk, until his own immunological system has developed and is ready to take over.

Dr G. J. Ebrahim, of London's Tropical Child Health Unit, once showed me how extraordinarily flexible and precise is this immunizing capacity of breastmilk. He asked me the name of the village where I lived.

'Penn,' I said, intrigued.

'Every locality,' he explained, 'has its own peculiar variety of the microbes causing infection. Well, the breastmilk you feed your baby with will have adjusted itself so that it will immunize your baby against the Penn variant – whereas a friend of yours in a nearby village will have developed a different variant, to protect her baby from the microbes in her locality.

'Calculate the amount of immunizing substances present in breastmilk and then go to the chemist and see just how much you would have to pay for that!'

To have its own personalized immunization system to hand is an amazing privilege for a baby – and essential for the baby who is likely to have no other. Health researchers in Guatemala, in the village of Santa Maria Cauque, found themselves in an environment lethal to new born babies: there was rampant infection, overcrowding, no immunization, little sanitation. And yet, they noted, not a single baby died – as long as the baby was of full birth-weight and had been breastfed.

It is a tragedy that artificial babymilk manufacturers should spend millions of dollars every year taking this solitary privilege away from the poor world's babies. A baby in a sanitized well-to-do environment may be able to manage without the constant protection breastmilk affords, but a baby brought up in a slum needs every scrap. Dr Ebrahim was unequivocal on this point. 'If I see a baby in a poor village being fed with a bottle,' he said grimly, 'I know I may as well reach in my pocket for a death certificate to sign.'

HEALTH FOOD FOR BABIES

Dietary advice keeps changing – except for one piece of information: that 'breast is best'. For a brief while, even this was hidden under a cloud, as four-hourly bottle-feeding became the fashionable regime to follow. Unfortunately, the fashion for bottle-feeding spread (deliberately, through heavy-duty marketing) from the middle classes in the North to poor families in the Third World. Rich infants didn't die in their hundreds of thousands because of bottle-feeding, although studies showed

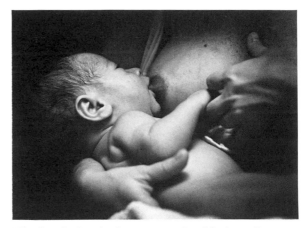

The battle for the breast: artificial babymilk manufacturers use slick advertising to persuade mothers to switch from breast to bottle.

that many did become more susceptible to gastric troubles and allergies: but among the poor, the consequences of bottle-feeding soon became a matter of public anxiety.

The trouble is that you need quite a high level of income to feed a baby reasonably safely on artificial babymilk. For a start, you need to be able to afford to buy enough of the formula: a lot of poor mothers cannot, so they eke out the fabulously expensive tins of formula by diluting it to make it go further. When the baby falls sick, undernourished by the weak mixture, the mother feeds the baby even less, in order not to tax his weak digestion. Unintentionally, she starves him to death.

You must also be able to afford to prepare the feed properly. If you live in an affluent society, then you are likely to have a fridge to keep the formula cool – bacteria love warm milk to breed in. You are also likely to have clean running water from a tap and an electric kettle or a stove for boiling water, and plenty of fuel to boil the water thoroughly; not to.mention time, equipment and fuel to sterilize all the feeding equipment, as well as more heat for warming up the formula when you take it out of the fridge. But this is a picture of the reality facing a

Third World mother, as researchers in central Yemen found:

Fetching water can involve a round trip to the spring or well of an hour or more, often in steep or mountainous country; and the fuel necessary for proper sterilisation of bottles and teats is scarce and prohibitively expensive. . . . The major cause of both the malnutrition and diarrhoea among the younger infants is probably bottle-feeding.

And fridges, needless to say, are not a normal household appliance in poor communities.

In their desire to do the best for their babies poor mothers reduce their own diets and the diets of other members of the family – after all, formula is what rich white people give their bouncing blond children, according to the advertisements. The result is hunger all round, paid for at very high cost. And the irony is that these mothers have, unknown to them, the world's best possible food available for their babies all the time. At very little expense, a mother could feed herself well – and then she would be able to manufacture the most delicious, nourishing food for the child in her own body. There would be two well-satisfied stomachs for the price of a scoopful of formula.

In 1981, after a vigorous campaign by activists all over the world, the World Health Assembly passed a resolution banning the advertising of artificial breastmilk substitutes. It hasn't stopped the sale, though it may have lowered its profile a little. What we need next is a parallel international campaign promoting breastfeeding – but that, of course, doesn't earn any commercial manufacturers a profit.

Breastmilk is a truly miraculous substance. Its superficial virtues are described in the old joke: 'It's always at the right temperature, the container's sterile, it's cheap – and the cat can't get at it.' But its subtler virtues are almost beyond belief. For a start, it is perfectly balanced, with the correct amount of nutrients for the baby, as long as the mother is adequately nourished (and that, as we have seen, doesn't have to cost much).

As the result of a worldwide bottle-feeding boom, thousands of babies die needlessly.

And then, ingeniously, breastmilk adjusts itself to the appropriate consistency: just after a baby is born, for instance, the breastmilk emerges in a thick, highly concentrated form called 'colostrum'. There is very little of it, but it is so rich that the newborn baby is well fed even when he is a novice at sucking. After a few days, when the baby has learned to suck strongly and deeply, the milk frees up its consistency and gushes out happily.

The breast also adjusts the quantity of milk that is required. If the baby is very hungry – or if the mother has had twins – the breast will produce a lot of milk. If the baby is a small eater who likes her food little and often, that's exactly what the breast will produce. The mother's breast and the baby's body understand each other wonderfully well. In hot weather (when his mother drinks more liquid), a baby will find a more thirst-quenching feed at the breast than he will in wintry weather. The richness of the milk also varies with the time of day – and even during the course of a feed: a baby's equivalent of a main course and a rich dessert may keep warm in one breast, while a drink to wash it down waits at the other. And when the baby starts to be weaned on to other foods and doesn't require so much milk, the breast cuts down on its production levels. All this happens without a word.

For centuries, all over the world, mothers and babies have communicated satisfyingly in this way through the wisdom of their bodies. But during the twentieth century, myths about breasts and breast-feeding spread through the modernized world. One cultural myth was that breasts were really only sexual playthings for men, nothing to do with babies and little to do even with the women to whom they belonged; breasts were treated as if they were 'screwed on' to female chests, their depersonalized mystique undisturbed by messy realities like leaking nipples. Dainty, deodorized modern women left such bovine activities to earthy peasant women, and reached for the bottle. Britt Ekland explained that she doesn't breastfeed her baby because it would interfere with her exercise routine.

One of the most powerful of these new myths was that many mothers 'couldn't' breastfeed. Mothers stopped doing what they had always managed to do naturally, and started to worry about it. Like the centipede who couldn't move once it had been asked whether it put its right foot forward first or its left, modern mothers worried themselves into self-fulfilling the 'not-enough-milk' prophecy. As a result of the worldwide bottle-feeding boom, paediatricians like Derrick Jelliffe of the Caribbean Food and Nutrition Institute in Jamaica estimated ten million babies a year suffered needlessly every year from malnutrition, and hundreds of thousands died.

The myth of maternal inadequacy was encouraged by manufacturers of artificial breastmilk substitutes. A spokesman for these manufacturers once assured me that they didn't move in on mothers immediately after childbirth – 'not until they have had a good chance to see if they could breastfeed'. Only when the mothers 'were sure they couldn't breastfeed', he said, did they provide them reassuringly with bottled formula.

And how long, I asked him, were these mothers given to find out if they were 'failures' or not?

'Oh, the whole of the first day,' he said. If the milk hadn't started to flow by then, the manufacturers felt justified in moving in with the bottle of infant formula.

Just one day? We know that breastmilk never does flow freely on the first day. These mothers aren't told about colostrum (though dairy farmers know all about its goodness and guard their cows' colostrum with care). Mothers are allowed to think that if they don't produce a gush straightaway, the sort you splash on cornflakes, they must be the 'failures' they've heard so much about.

Salespersons were even dressed up, cynically, in uniforms that made them look like nurses, and then sent to poor villages to promote infant formula. The babyfoods action network (in one of the most successful protests mounted by concerned members of the public, supported by UNICEF and WHO) managed to stop these grosser infringements of the right of infants to their proper source of nourishment and immunization. Even enormous commercial interests can be deflected, if there is enough clarity and conviction in those who act together to counter the force of commercial greed. But vigilance is needed and the Nestlé Boycott of the 1970s and early 1980s is on again.

One more thing. In the West, women rarely breastfeed their babies for more than a year, often not more than a few months. There is some embarrassment about older infants suckling (as though it's a habit they should have 'grown out of' by seven or eight months old) perhaps linked to the embarrassed modern equation of breasts with sex toys. But elsewhere in the world, children come to their mothers for a comforting suckle at three and four years of age. The average age for children to stop breastfeeding, worldwide, has been estimated to be around two-and-a-half years.

And in some societies it is said that husbands do not expect to have sexual intercourse with wives who are feeding their babies. This means that for a space of two or three years, the women are free of pregnancy – the correct time to elapse for babies to be born 'not too close' for maternal and child health. Even in societies where this custom is not practised, breastfeeding itself provides a degree of contraceptive protection during the first few months while the mother is feeding the baby solely on her own milk; the baby's strong sucking triggers a contraceptive hormone. So birth-spacing, too, is encouraged naturally (though not infallibly) by breastfeeding.

In effect, the child health network set up by human agencies imitates and complements the network that Nature has already introduced through the breast. Breastfeeding reminds us that babies need to be fed appropriately and cleanly; that babies need to be immunized; that childbirth should be spaced two or three years apart; that babies need flexible and sensitive responses from their parents; and that babies deserve the best care the world has to offer – all babies, equally.

4

THE WOLF AT THE DOOR

Billions of dollars were irresponsibly lent and irresponsibly borrowed. Yet now, when the party's over, it is the poor who are being asked to pay . . . And by far the heaviest consequences are being borne by children.

James Grant, UNICEF

Mary Nti and John Oppong live with their four small sons – Steven, Paul, Ernest and Gabriel – in the remote village of Ntinanko, in the Ashanti region of Ghana. They own two acres of farmland, most of which is devoted to cocoa. 'Cocoa has become a national priority,' John Oppong says. 'I have taken cocoa farming seriously. I intend concentrating on my farming activities so as to earn enough to ensure the children's upkeep for the future.'

John Oppong is anxious that his children should have a sound start in life – and in this the Convention on the Rights of the Child supports him. The Convention establishes the right of all children to have (at the very least) their basic needs met: their right to food, clean water, health care, shelter, education . . . But it has not been easy for the majority of parents in poor countries to provide these essentials for their children and in recent years it has been getting harder than ever: for poor countries have been getting poorer still during the 1980s. After 40 years of gradual improvement, the developing world has begun to get poorer again.

'For almost nine hundred million people, approximately one-sixth of humankind,' says the 1989 State of the World's Children Report, 'the march of human progress has now become a retreat. Large areas of the world are sliding backwards into poverty.' And that means the poorest families in the world sliding down into the very depths of a poverty which can barely sustain life. In the past 12 months alone, half a million children have given up their fragile hold on life and slipped into oblivion because of this downturn in their countries' economies. Villagers like John and Mary know that it would not take much misfortune to reduce their family to penury – and that this misfortune would arise from sources beyond their control.

Mary says: We dare not hope. It takes five years for the cocoa trees to mature. But even when they ripen and you sell the cocoa, the amount you get buys only one piece of cloth and the money is gone. What we need is an increase in the price of cocoa, so we can have more income to provide for our children.' And despite John's brave words about ensuring his children's upkeep, he knows there are problems. 'The capital I have is not sufficient to keep up my work,' he admits. 'Those of us who are cocoa farming are going through a painful period of time. We should be given great care by the

51

government in terms of the price, so that we could depend on the money to keep our family better.'

GLOBAL PARENTS

John and Mary's four sons live at the centre of a series of concentric circles. The children's immediate circle consists of the family, and the family has a responsibility to provide the children with their basic needs. But the family lives within the larger circle of the state – and the state governs the economic climate within which the family operates. If a government decides, say, to increase interest rates or to allow high unemployment, these national policy choices will powerfully affect the ability of the family circle to protect the child within it. If, as a

Mary Nti and John Oppong with three sons.

result, the family income is smaller in real terms today than yesterday, then members of the government – the 'parents' of the nation – must take responsibility for the family's hardship.

But even the government doesn't make free choices: there is another concentric circle within which the government operates – the circle of international finance. Who are the decision-makers in the outermost circle? We have not elected them. We do not even know their names. But these 'global parents' need to be included in any consideration of family welfare, for their decisions are matters of life and death to children.

John has a vague sense (as much as most of us) of this powerful outer circle. 'I don't know much about sending cocoa abroad,' he says. But: 'Those abroad should be in a better position to help us – so that we can help them. We want them to negotiate a better price with the government, so that the government would also be in a better position to give more money to us – to maintain our lives and for us to maintain the industry.'

He is anxious to cooperate with every layer of this system of concentric circles so that the system works to everyone's benefit. But are the 'global parents' in the powerful outer circle as cooperatively minded as he is? Are they even aware of the vulnerable members of the global family in the innermost circle, like John, Mary and their four small sons?

John Oppong and Mary Nti depend utterly on earning a good price for their cocoa. And that price is not controlled by them, nor even by their government: it is fixed by the outer circle. World commodity prices rise and fall, guided – we are told – by the Invisible Hand of market forces. And on this Hand the fate of the family in Ntinanko depends. However hard the family works to grow cocoa, however successful they are, they cannot guarantee a good living. For that, they are dependent on the whims of the Hand.

The Hand has for several years kept cocoa prices pressed firmly under its thumb. Cocoa has been selling for a song – and so have many of the poor

Neither the family nor their government controls the price of cocoa.

THE HUNGRY MAW

The rich are the world's great consumers. Even though they make up only a quarter of the world's people, they eat their way through three-quarters of the world's resources; they are the people with the money to go shopping. And when the rich lose interest in a product, the producers lose their customers. Their own people are too poor to buy such goods – how many Ghanaian villagers could afford a bar of chocolate made with Ghanaian cocoa? – and their fellows in poverty, the other poor nations, are in the same boat. None of them can afford to buy what the others can no longer sell.

Another reason offered for the slump in Third World commodity prices is that there is a glut. Farmers like John and Mary have worked to grow as much cocoa as possible, backed by efforts from the government and advice from international economists. But sometimes it seems as if all this hard work is thrown back in the farmers' faces: too much cocoa, they are told, lowers prices. The North has so much cheap chocolate to wade through that it is becoming seriously worried about its waistline.

In Ghana, the serious worries have been about child malnutrition. In Ntinanko, UNICEF workers have helped the parents by building a mill in which the mothers grind nuts and corn for a weaning mix which they feed their youngest children. As a result, Mary's youngest son, she says, has grown visibly sturdier than the others. But UNICEF cannot build mills in every village and, in any case, parents don't want their children's lives or deaths to depend on charity. They want reasonable prices, reasonably guaranteed, for the hard work they have done. But the only way Ghana's families have survived is because the Ghanaian government has borrowed huge sums of money from Northern bankers.

Apart from Africa, the part of the world most deeply affected by economic decline is Latin America. In the poor north-east of Brazil, for instance, infant mortality rose by 20 per cent in just two years, as hungry mothers gave birth to babies too fragile and

world's other commodities, like copper, cotton and rubber. At times prices rise – but not because the growers are in a position to demand higher prices. They can do little but work hard – and hope. But even small fluctuations can spell disaster for families that are balanced precariously on the edge of survival.

One reason offered by the international economists for the frequent low prices is that there is a less certain market for many of the Third World's commodities at present. But why this lack of interest? One of the reasons is that the rich world has found substitutes for some of the commodities – artificial sweeteners for sugar; synthetic fabrics for cotton – and doesn't need them as much any more.

Brazil is one of the world's largest debtors: and its children suffer the consequences.

undernourished to survive. And nutritionists are worried about an epidemic of dwarfism in this area.

What about aid? There is a common misconception in the industrialized world that the Third World is a vast and hungry maw into which the more advanced countries pour all the material goodness they can spare. Some people in these countries think the poor are mainly financed by the rich, and resent the massive subsidy they imagine that they are providing. Reality is quite otherwise. There is very little real aid given by the rich world to the poor. Even its long-promised commitment to give just 0.7 per cent of the GNP in aid has not yet materialized: it gives barely half that amount. *If the rich world kept its promise every child could be guaranteed her or his basic needs.* The poor consume very little – they haven't the money to buy more. To raise their standard of living a fraction wouldn't cost the rich much – but that fraction could make the difference between poor children living or dying. But giving even a little more aid is not on the rich world's present agenda.

On the contrary, even the aid that is given often boomerangs back to the donor country. Over half of the official aid from the West is 'tied': that is, it is conditional on the poor country using the money to buy expensive goods that the rich country wants to sell. Unscrupulous nineteenth-century factory-owners paid their workers in vouchers that could only be cashed at the owners' high-price stores. Tied loans are a disturbing echo. In the case of the United Kingdom, 75 per cent of official bilateral aid (that is, government-to-government aid) is tied to the purchase of British goods and services.

So what the rich world gives with its left hand, it takes away with its right. In fact, its right hand scoops away more than the left hand offers. The vast maw that is being fed belongs to the rich world, not the poor.

In 1983, when the Ethiopian famine hit the world's headlines, members of the public reached deep into their pockets in an unprecedented act of individual generosity. But in the same year Ethiopia paid out to the West four times as much as the public gave in charity. The money could – and should – have been spent on saving the starving. In fact, it was used for debt repayments to bankers who had no trouble, it seems, in accepting it. In 1988, the sum that flowed North from the South as a whole was, on a conservative estimate, $20 billion more than flowed the other way. On average, a quarter of the poor world's export revenues flowed North in repayments.

So the poor are financing the rich. How could such a bizarre situation come about?

DEBT: THE WOLF AT THE DOOR

The poor world's economy is sick. Paralysed down one side, it languishes lopsidedly like a damaged seal, unable to swim after its scattered children. The paralysis is caused by twin pincers squeezing its spinal cord. One pincer is low income, because of depressed commodity prices. The other is the burden of debt.

Debt repayments are the chief obstacle to improving the developing world's economy. If it is to become healthy enough to implement the rights of its children to their basic needs, it needs to be free of this paralysing burden. Until then, it will go on sending interest payments, never able to clear itself of debt. Exporting all this money means the developing world is unable to oil the wheels of industry and agriculture, so that it grows poorer still. It also means cutting back on family welfare programmes, and this hits the poor hardest. Parents watch helplessly as their children fade and die – and all the time their governments keep sending money to the North.

Why did poor countries get themselves into this

When interest rates were low, governments borrowed heavily to finance prestige projects and modern urban development.

fix in the first place, borrowing money they cannot now repay? Many of us are torn between sympathy for their plight – they are, after all, very poor, and we don't want babies to die for the sake of money – and irritation. Why shouldn't these countries honour their debts like anyone else? If we ran up a huge debt on our credit card, the creditors wouldn't let us off. Even those who believe that mercy should temper justice may feel that, this time, justice stands on the side of the creditors.

According to James Grant, the debtor countries certainly showed some irresponsibility. They were careless with some of the loan money and took a gamble with the rest – a gamble that didn't pay off. But the responsibility cannot be placed entirely at their door. In the 1970s, when banks were awash with petro-dollars, they were pressing poor countries to borrow large sums. Unlike friends, who lend each other money with sympathetic anxiety, banks *prefer* people to be in debt to them – that's how they make their money. Banks offered credit on easy terms to the poor countries: and they accepted it gladly.

Borrowing seemed sensible at the time. Money was cheap because interest rates were low and inflation was high. The choice facing the Third World was not unlike the choice facing an engaged couple who have found a marital home they want to buy, though they can't afford it outright. If they wait until they have saved up the present asking price, the inflation will put the house out of their reach again. So it would be more sensible to buy the house now, especially if interest rates are low, borrowing the rest of the money and promising to pay mortgage repayments every month. What the Third World wanted to buy was their way into the 'modern' trade system. Industrialization cost a lot but it was widely touted as the way forward to prosperity. While money was cheap it made sense to borrow and buy – and pay back their 'mortgage' every month with the new profits they would make.

The trouble was that when it came to repaying the debts, money was no longer cheap. Interest rates had gone up. (Or rather – we need to watch out for economists' euphemisms – they had not 'gone up', as if by some act of God, they had been 'put up' by people.) And at the same time, the prosperity that was supposed to come from the investment in industry didn't materialize, partly due to the high price of oil, partly due to management failures, but mainly due to the slump in commodity prices.

Tanzania, for example, was shocked by the price of cotton dropping from 68 cents per pound to 34 cents *in one day*. How was Tanzania to repay her debt now? President Julius Nyerere cried out to the world: 'Must we starve our children to pay our debts?'

THE LOST GENERATION

Children are disproportionately at risk when a country is in trouble for two reasons. As the most vulnerable members of society, they are the first to show symptoms of suffering and the least able to bear them – a baby will die of hunger sooner than a man. Secondly, as the least-empowered members of society, children must usually wait for adults to protect them. Unfortunately, even politicians who are fond of claiming that children are 'mankind's greatest investment' or 'its most precious resource' tend to forget this rhetoric under pressure and reach for short-term answers. Industry appears, in the short term, to earn the country money and protecting children to cost money. So industry gets the money and child welfare programmes are cut back – temporarily, of course, just until the day when economic recovery makes them affordable once more. At times like this, politicians decide that morality is a luxury: monetarism sounds more 'realistic'.

But, as we saw in the previous chapter, children cannot afford to wait; and a government cannot afford to cure later at great cost what it cannot afford to prevent for a fraction of that cost now.

Children depend on families — but family incomes have shrunk by 10–25 per cent in Latin America and Africa during the 1980s.

Latin Americans talk of a 'lost generation' as family welfare programmes become the first victims of economic cutbacks. The 40 least developed countries have slashed spending on health by 50 per cent and on education by 25 per cent over the past few years, in an effort to tighten national belts so that they can keep industry going while paying their debts. In almost half of the developing countries, the proportion of six- to eleven-year-olds in school is falling. A World Health Organization representative has said that in more than 50 per cent of cases, African governments cut spending in the health sector first.

Nor can poor families replace from their own earnings what their governments no longer provide. Family incomes have been shrinking by 10–25 per cent in Africa and Latin America, because employers are, naturally, reluctant to increase wages at a time of economic recession and rising prices. But as wages stagnate, costs are rising for families. The fastest prices to rise are usually for food. At the same time subsidies on basic foodstuffs have been abolished. The poorer a family is, the larger the proportion of their income they spend on food, so food price rises and subsidy cuts hit the poorest hardest. Life is always the most expensive for those who can least afford the expense.

In rural areas, some of the poor manage to grow their own food, and they are at least sheltered from one expense. But they are vulnerable to cuts in other basic services like health and education – and if they earn their livelihood as farmers, they are faced with rising transport costs and decreasing markets.

What compounds the tragedy is that many of these human sacrifices seem to have been made in vain. Mysteriously, even the Third World countries that have followed hard-nosed economic prescriptions to the letter have not found their economies recovering, or not for long. A brief upturn at huge social cost was not what the developing countries' governments had in mind when they made their painful choices to set aside human welfare for economic recovery.

GHANA'S STORY

The government of Ghana, for example, decided to listen to the tough advice of international economists from the International Monetary Fund (IMF) and the World Bank when its economy was in serious trouble in 1983. Ghana had not always been poor. In the decade following independence in 1957, Ghana had been an economic success. It was the world's largest producer of cocoa and had one of the highest per capita incomes in West Africa. But its economy has gone into a long downhill slide in the past two decades, fuelled by worsening trade terms – including the rise in oil prices. Between 1975 and 1983, the minimum real wage declined by 86 per cent; child malnutrition and infant mortality soared. In 1983, Ghana hit rock bottom after suffering the worst drought in living memory; bush fires raged across the parched land destroying cocoa trees; low water levels at the Akosombo dam on the Volta river halved electricity supplies to industry; and more than a million Ghanaians arrived on Ghana's doorstep, deported en masse from Nigeria.

That was the last straw. In desperation, Ghana's government turned to the advice of Northern experts – and duly cut food subsidies, made tens of thousands of workers redundant, devalued its currency (2.75 cedis bought a dollar in 1983, but it takes 280 cedis to buy a dollar in 1988); sold off state-owned plantations and poured borrowed money into improving cocoa production and export. Other ways of raising money included introducing 'cost recovery measures' into the health and education service, a euphemism for fees. A further job-loss programme – excising 45,000 jobs from the civil service over three years – began in 1987.

The package of cuts was known to everyone as the 'austerity programme' – to everyone, that is, except the economists, who have another obscuring euphemism for it: 'structural adjustment programme' or (perhaps more appropriately) SAP. Some people have welcomed the changes. The civil servants that

Dangerously dependent on cocoa, Ghana cannot now afford to diversify its economy.

With all this borrowing to refinance the cocoa industry, Ghana's external debt has almost doubled since 1983. 'Much of this,' writes Tony Hodges of *Africa Recovery* magazine, 'is unreschedulable debt contracted from the World Bank and the IMF, some of it in the IMF's case on relatively hard terms.' In other words, these debts must be repaid straightaway. In 1987, Hodges continues:

27% of Ghana's exports of goods and services went to paying debt service to the IMF alone, and the total debt service ratio rose to 63%. These ratios will be even higher [in 1988] because of both increased debt service requirements and the fall in export earnings.

So the chances of Ghana ever clearing its debt recede into expensive infinity as long as its main source of foreign exchange brings in little, and then less, income. While Ghana's government cannot control the price at which cocoa sells on the international commodity markets, cocoa can no longer be relied on to bring Ghana enough income.

What is there left now in Ghana to sacrifice? How much more can the government ask its people to tighten their belts? At present, the minimum wage of US 63 cents a day will not buy a tuber of yam – even for those lucky enough to be employed. It seems that the people of Ghana must now depend on aid from rich well-wishers and on the hope that its debts will be 'forgiven' – an undignified term that makes Ghana sound like a nation of spendthrifts rather than a nation of people that have cooperated in sacrifice.

Nor can Ghana's farmers diversify, so that they become less dependent on cocoa sales. To switch to a new crop, as John Oppong and Mary Nti know, costs money – and time: five years perhaps before the fields are re-planted and new crops mature. Poor people cannot wait that long. Having spent so much on producing cocoa, Ghana must now, it seems, stay locked in the cocoa business.

So have the sacrifices made by the people in so many of the Third World's countries, like Ghana,

remain in work, for instance, are to be paid more. But what about those who now have no income at all?

Despite all these drastic measures, Ghana's future is not assured. Tsatsu Tsikata of Ghana's National Economic Commission says bleakly: 'The current decline in cocoa prices is depriving Ghana of significant resources that structural adjustment efforts had anticipated when they were embarked upon.' In other words, all this effort and sacrifice by Ghanaians is counteracted by the low cocoa prices ordained by the international trading system.

However much responsibility an individual country takes to improve its industry or to curb public spending, it is still disabled by a world trading system in which it has virtually no say.

Children have become the victims of economic restraints as governments in the poorest countries cut health programmes by half and education programmes by a quarter.

to rally their national economy been worth it? And who asked the children – or their parents – in these countries if these were the sacrifices they wanted to make? To what extent did the people who have the final power to make decisions about global finance take into account their effects on children?

Ghana's head of state, Flt Lt Jerry Rawlings, speaks with understandable bitterness:

Our children have become the unfortunate victims of the economic restraints of our countries. Their lives are constrained by the indebtedness of the countries in which they live . . . We are obliged to market their future.

Third World countries are not merely destined to service the demands of the industrialized countries at prices which they dictate for our products. Nor do we wish to become the recipients of handouts from the industrial countries. We want to earn reasonable prices for our products to live in dignity with enough income to provide for the basic needs of our children.

The international commodities market continually devalues our efforts and erodes our resources. . . . We must all come to terms with the blunt truth that a disadvantaged child in a cocoa growing village . . . cannot have substantially improved opportunities unless developed countries make concerted efforts to narrow the gap between rich and poor countries . . . Unless we solve these problems, the call for human rights, the talk about democracy, becomes meaningless.

THE 'FREE' MARKET

Economists who advocate free market forces say that in an interdependent world everyone plays the same money game. Their critics question whether there can be genuine interdependence between unequals; or can there only be exploitation by the stronger players of the weaker ones? After all, what say do Mary Nti and John Oppong have in deciding a fair price for their cocoa? Absolutely none. And yet their livelihood could be destroyed at any moment by anonymous accountants in the outer circle.

Christian Aid's analysts add a further argument: that the market is only kept 'free' when it suits powerful members of the North. In *Banking on the Poor*, their analysis of the ethics of Third World debt, they point out that:

When big corporations like Chrysler in the USA and Jaguar in the UK have been threatened with bankruptcy, they have been provided with rescue packages . . . and most important of all, the recognition that the company must be allowed to return to growth and profitability if it is to recover. Few such concessions have been made to the developing countries which have been expected to bear the full burden . . . [under] market conditions.

What is important for us to note, in the context of children's rights, is the potent relationship between the outermost circle and the innermost circle where children live – for this relationship is vital, although it has been unrecognized for so long. Our children have been invisible to the bankers, as the bankers have been invisible to us. With the awakening awareness of the global dimension of children's rights, all those who pull the global purse-strings must now be consciously included, for they have a crucial part to play in honouring the child's right to basic needs.

Ask a roomful of adults to name the leaders of four of the world's most powerful states and they will usually manage it. Ask if, in their opinion, these leaders have power over our lives – and the answer is likely to be yes. But ask who heads the World Bank or the International Monetary Fund, or any of the other major financial institutions of the world, or the largest multinational corporations, and they are likely to respond with a baffled silence.

It is hard to put pressure on people of whose existence we hardly know. As they are unelected, we have no power to rescind their authority; the first rule of democracy is broken and we are reduced to mice playing between cats' paws. But we must not forget that our ignorance of *their* lives does not prevent them having power over *our* lives. We need to insist that these faceless decision-makers take their share of responsibility for the welfare of the world's children.

With such an arbitrary and remote relationship between them and us, it seems likely that they would be more aware of economic growth – which they look at every day – than the growth of people whom they do not know. Professor Reginald Green, of the Institute of Development Studies at Sussex University, UK, says he does not believe that the World Bank and the IMF deliberately set out to design their programmes to aggravate inequality and poverty but that 'The Bank, and especially the Fund, do often find the poor and vulnerable to be invisible'.

Third World economists are less benign in their assessment of the bankers' motives, whether they are commercial or development bankers. Akilagpa Sawyerr, the Vice-Chancellor of Ghana's university, sees the North's economic policies as a form of neo-colonialism. He says that structural adjustment programmes entrench a poor country's dependence on external capital, while failing to mobilize domestic human and material resources: 'Aid and the debt trap constitute the carrot and the stick by which the industrialised countries seek to bend Third World countries to their will.' Susan George, in *A Matter of Life and Debt*, agrees. She sees the concept of the 'free' market as a rationalization which allows the rich to watch the poor countries starve, and then buy up their assets at a marked-down price – a form of silent colonialism without need of missiles and missionaries.

Either way, intentionally or not, it is clear that the bankers have been more aware of the dollar signs before their eyes than the signs of human distress all around them.

WASTERS OF THE PLANET'S WEALTH

Such shortsightedness is destructive to everyone in the long run. The effects of the economic recession in the Third World are now spreading to industrial countries. It has been estimated that two million jobs in the United States have been lost as a result of lost trade.

The Third World's debt was, in 1988, a staggering *trillion* dollars – that is $1,000 billion. But the world spends $900 billion every year on military expenditure, according to the Pate Institute for Human Survival. That's approximately $2,500,000,000 *every day*. And Carl Sagan of Cornell University estimates in *Earth Conference One* (Shambhala, 1989) that a further half a trillion dollars is spent each year in the United States on drug dealing. So the money is there, but at present being spent on weapons that can never be used, or on drugs that wreck lives, rather than on saving the Third World from deepening destitution.

American warplanes wait to be exported to the developing world.

Since 1945, says Sagan, the United States has spent 10 trillion dollars on the Cold War. 'What could you buy with 10 trillion dollars?' he asks. 'The answer is – everything; everything except the land; every skyscraper, house, ship, train, airplane, automobile, baby diaper, pencil, everything could be purchased for 10 trillion dollars.' And he gives an example of money better spent: 'Smallpox has been eliminated from the planet: the cost was one hour of the global military budget.'

People who waste the world's wealth are very easy to find in the debtor countries too. Twenty families (around 100 guests) were recently invited to stay the weekend at one of Sri Lanka's sumptuous tourist hotels, lying around the pool and sipping drinks; it was just a little treat to celebrate the host's fortieth birthday. These families are not aristocrats or billionaires: they are ordinary middle-class merchants. Since these Third World elites often feel they have more in common with the elites of the North than with the poor of their birthplaces, you can also find them flying casually back and forth between 'home' and Europe or America. In the meantime, the minimum daily wage 'back home' has crawled up to 50 Sri Lankan rupees: less than US $2 a day.

'Capital flight' is the term given to capital that has been flown out of the South (sometimes literally, crammed into airline flightbags) and into Northern banks by these 'brown sahibs' who bleed their countries as surely as did their white colonialist predecessors. The banks welcome the cash: the money they had lent to the developing country has now flown back to its nest, so that the bankers can lend it again – quite possibly to the same country – to make a second profit on the same sum. Ex-President Marcos of the Philippines is reputed to have cost his country in personal expenses at least 15 per cent of its 26 billion dollar debt. Sometimes the Third World's money reappears in tax-exempt offshore banks. The rich bankers of the North and their rich customers from the South do well for themselves.

'Back home', leaders pour money into prestige projects – status symbols like huge stadia or statues. Buying military weapons and paying army salaries, to show the leaders' enemies (external and internal) how powerful they are, can consume a further 10–20 per cent of a developing country's borrowings. The payment for these military weapons also flies North, to the rich countries that manufacture them.

But even after all this financial mismanagement – to put it politely – the bulk of the money usually remains. What is left is invested in the world trading system by producing capital-intensive export commodities – at the expense of small-scale rural development schemes that empower communities and can be replicated by poor people themselves at little cost. But why has it been so hard for developing countries to do what the North managed during the Industrial Revolution? If large-scale industrialization worked in the North, why doesn't it work in the South?

Industrializing the North was also costly in human terms. But the North could prosper because it held the world's power balance in its favour: colonization meant it could extract raw materials at pitifully cheap rates, like cotton from India to feed Lancashire mills. In the process of industrializing the

North exploited the South. But the poor countries of the South that are developing modern production systems in the twentieth century still have the world's power balance working against them: instead of access to cheap resources, they have to buy exorbitantly expensive materials from the rich world, like chemical pesticides, fertilizer, or spare parts for machinery. In the process of industrializing the South, the South is exploited once more. Whoever has the power has always made the profit.

CONTROLLING INTEREST

And yet, despite their falling incomes, despite the catastrophic social costs, the countries of the poor world do keep on honouring their debts. On average, debt repayments now claim nearly a quarter of the developing world's export revenues. Far from being careless about paying back the sums they borrowed, many of the debtor countries have long since paid back the equivalent of the principal – several times over.

It isn't the principal that causes the problem: it is the secondary sum caused by the bloating creature called 'interest'. If one year you have a lean harvest and cannot pay, it doesn't pity your plight; it waits, distending, licking its lips, while you grow thinner. Any delay means feeding it bigger portions later.

In ancient times, when agriculture was the norm and everyone understood the vagaries of the storm god and the fertility goddess, the law made allowances for lean years. The Code of Hammurabi (*c.* 2250 BC) says:

If a man owe a debt and [the storm god] inundate his field and take away the produce, or if through lack of water grain has not grown in the field, in that year he shall not make any return of grain to the creditor; he shall alter his contract-tablet and he shall not pay the interest for that year.

But now the world – or at least, that part of the world that calls the tune – is no longer sensitive to the weather or to the people whose lives rise and fall with the rhythm of the seasons. The demands for debt repayments issue with mechanical regularity from a culture where every month jerks flatly on like any other. After all, the factories of the industrialized world grind out their wares whatever the weather. There is no respite. Lending with interest used to be called usury, and was against the law in certain cultures. Now the law is on the side of the creditor and his unwavering demands.

So the bankers of the West, to use the metaphor of *The Merchant of Venice*, have long since had their shipments of gold returned; what they are waiting for now are the pounds of flesh they felt they had a 'right' to, if the gold is not paid back at once.

The question we have to ask ourselves is this: at what point do we counter the written rules of the commercial system with the unwritten rules of a humane society? It is a cliché of British history books that 200 years ago a man could be arrested and deported to Australia for stealing an apple for his hungry children. He *has* broken a commercial rule – he has taken an apple without paying its market cost – but the human cost by which he repays his 'debt to society' we now consider to be too great. Deportation cannot be equal to the value of an apple.

And we are also aware that there is another uncomfortable issue here, beyond the price of apples. We may feel justified in punishing the man for behaving 'irresponsibly', but we also know that he is obeying a deeper responsibility: to keep his children alive. We are aware that, as members of the larger circle, we have failed to fulfil our responsibility to feed, or to enable this father to feed, his hungry children.

Today we are still faced with this dilemma. We know that 'responsible' behaviour requires commercial promises being kept by the debtor countries – apples should be paid for; but we know we have other promises to keep. Which should our priority be – to keep our promises to the bankers or

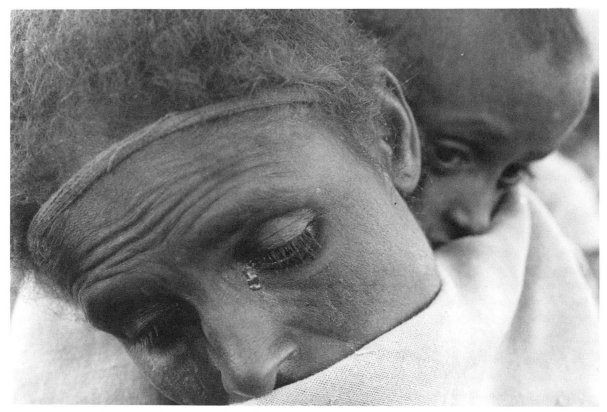

What price can be put on human suffering?

our promise to look after hungry children? In time, of course, we may be able to do both. But which should our first priority be?

The reality is that we have chosen, just as in the eighteenth century, to pay for the apples at the cost of the children.

THE UNACCEPTABLE FACE OF ADJUSTMENT

But a change is in the air. Some industrialized countries have begun to reduce the pressure they place on the developing world – for example, Italy, Canada and Scandinavia have now scaled down the

interest rates they charge Mozambique. And France has cancelled a third of Mozambique's debt. 'The Soviet Union,' writes Victoria Brittain, 'the creditor for one quarter of the total Mozambique debt, has made the humane gesture of simply cancelling all interest payments.'

The World Bank has at last set up a special unit to look at the social costs of economic policies. And the IMF's 'adjustment' programmes have been challenged by UNICEF in *Adjustment with a Human Face*. Its co-author, Richard Jolly, has been making a two-pronged attack on the IMF's neglect of social costs, one on economic and one on moral grounds. He begins with the economic argument. 'If you're concerned to strengthen investment in the future,' he says, 'it is a total contradiction in terms to be allowing half the population to be malnourished.

'To miss the human dimension . . . is an economic error. . . . To fail to protect young children at the critical stages of their growth is to wreak lasting damage on a whole generation, the results of which may well have effects on economic development and welfare for decades ahead.' This pragmatic argument has evidently been impressing the economists. The Managing Director of the IMF in 1986 conceded that 'human capital is after all the most important factor of production in developing and industrial countries alike'.

So is the unacceptable face of adjustment now to have a smile on it? In Ghana, there is to be a new economic programme called Programme of Actions to Mitigate the Social Cost of Adjustment (PAMS-CAD). But, as Richard Jolly points out, this programme doesn't replace the old strategy: it merely adds to it, carefully avoiding 'any *distortions* to the wider goals of the Economic Recovery Programme' (my italics). In other words, human welfare is seen as a 'distortion'; what is still considered inviolable is the economic plan.

Tarzie Vittachi has no time for tactfully re-adjusting adjustment programmes. He protests:

We need to go in with guns blazing. These are children's lives that are being destroyed! If we start talking about a little adjustment here, a little mitigation there, what we're doing is accepting the values of the people who run this system. We're falling under their spell – kowtowing to them – being cravenly grateful if they acknowledge us, by allowing us to change the system a little here and there. We're glad to get their smile of approval . . . That's the way to keep the system going, not the way to change it.

The real question is this: Is money the most important, the most solid reality for us? Or is the suffering of children, and the suffering of parents who cannot find the money to find their children food, just as solid and important a reality?

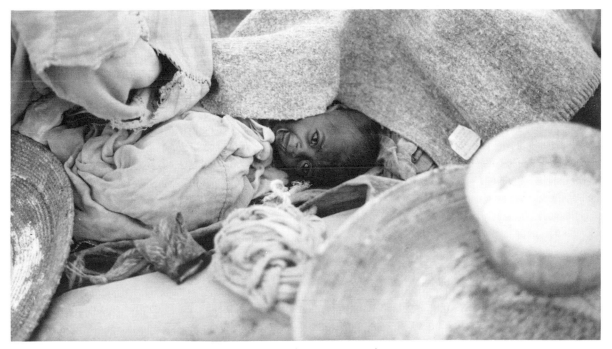

A tiny Ethiopian famine victim, frightened and alone, screams his misery.

Seeing a debt as an intractable reality is an easy trap to fall into. Money's special seduction is that it bears the illusion of stability. Ideas and ideals are known to be nebulous – they are shifty and unreliable: but 'currency' can seem 'hard'. In an unstable world where everything shifts, money at least seems to be fixed: it reassures with psychological as well as physical security.

But it is not true. Money never was and never will be a hard and fast commodity, any more than an idea or an ideal. It is as amorphous as smoke – and like smoke it can choke a man to death and then disappear silently into thin air. I asked a banker who specializes in Latin American investment why she enjoys her work. She described the satisfaction of saving a company on the edge of bankruptcy; it is now opening up a new branch. How did she bring about this transformation? Largely by re-labelling the amount it owed, allocating it to different accounting headings. Ask any accountant – money is malleable and has a thousand names.

Richard Jolly adds that Western countries have often had debts in the past – like the United States in the nineteenth century, when it was industrializing – but those debts have dissolved and no stigma remains. And he reminds us that after the Second World War the United States was happy to give Europe a hefty loan under the Marshall Plan – 2 per cent of its GNP in a support programme – knowing that a bankrupt Europe would be bad for world trade. Today, when the United States is much wealthier, the percentage of its GNP it gives in overseas aid is just 0.22 per cent.

Why is debt, when it is incurred by starving Africans, physically intractable and morally dubious? Jolly's answer is uncompromising:

I think the public does not understand the issues in clear terms. I think they tend often to see Africa's problems as the result of Africans, and there is some racism in that. People think Africans can't cope. But if you go back to the 1960s, post Independence, they achieved economic growth rates very impressively.

So if the stumbling-block is racism, we are dealing with a moral rather than economic problem. The debt crisis, in the end, has very little to do with the superficial 'reality' of money and everything to do with the underlying reality of human values.

Providing the basic needs of all human children is the responsibility of all humanity.

Jolly's moral argument in favour of economic programmes that put children first, then, is at least as substantial as his 'hard-headed' economic one:

How many of us would countenance rising malnutrition among our own children – without taking or demanding drastic and urgent remedial action? How many of us would be willing to accept for our own families a period of austerity so severe as to cause rising malnutrition among our own children? If our personal answers are so clear, can we not work together in an urgent search for alternatives internationally?

A WAY FORWARD

Poor countries could simply refuse to pay back the debt – and many are tempted to do so. But the North retaliates with a threat: if you default, we won't buy any of your goods and you'll be hungrier than ever. If enough Third World countries defaulted in unison, this blackmail might not work. But threat and counter-threat is a dangerous game.

Two gentler proposals are more favoured now. They build on the growing awareness of the world's interconnectedness. One proposal is that debt repayments should be set against money used to protect the environment – like saving tropical rain forests. Costa Rica has already started to put this proposal into practice, and the idea is catching on. People are beginning to see that though the trees may grow in one part of the planet, they benefit the whole of the world: therefore the planet as a whole should pay to keep the trees alive.

In the same way, a suggestion has been made that the planetary family should pay to keep its children safe. Debt repayments should be set against money used to look after children – so if a debtor country agreed to spend, say, 50 million dollars on child health care, the global community would agree to reduce its debt demand by the same amount. The proposal ignores the question of global inequity in its trading system, of course; but it may help to save another generation of the world's children being lost while this fundamental problem is being worked out.

It might also establish more firmly in the world's consciousness two principles that are essential if we are to honour the rights of children. The first is that money should always be spent to save the world's children, never children to save the world's money. And the second is that providing the basic needs of all human children is the responsibility of all humanity.

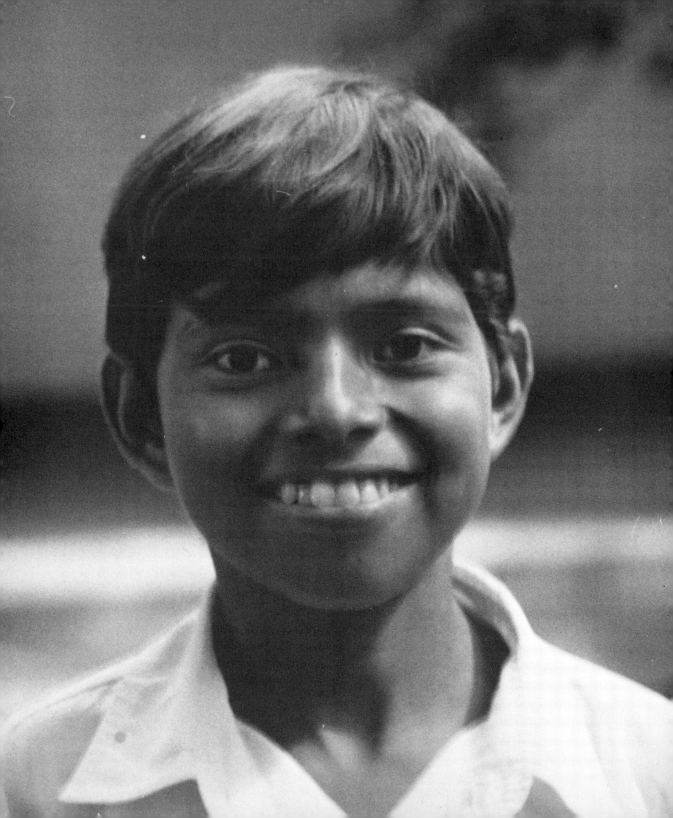

5

A CHANCE TO GO TO SCHOOL

A child's mind is not a vessel to be filled but a fire to be kindled.

Attributed to Confucius

Manuel Vilches, aged 12, lives in Tipitapa, Nicaragua. 'In order to start school at 7 a.m.,' he says, 'I catch the bus at 5 a.m.' After two bus rides, he walks the last part of the journey to school. He has lessons till three o'clock, before the long journey home. 'I take the buses back to Tipitapa. There I do my mother's commissions, and after dinner I go straight to bed.'

It's a long day for a young boy – but families place a high priority on education in Nicaragua. So does the Nicaraguan government. Despite the war and the country's poverty, Nicaragua is struggling to ensure that children like Manuel get the chance to learn.

Fifteen days after the Sandinista victory in 1979 and the overthrow of the Somoza dictatorship, a programme known as the 'Second Insurrection' was launched. The first insurrection had been the political one: a second, educational revolution had to follow, the Sandinistas believed, or the people would not become masters of their own fate.

Between 1979 and 1984, 4,000 classrooms were built for children – and a National Literacy Crusade was launched to educate their parents. The whole country was mobilized. Ninety-six thousand volunteers, mainly young, more than half of them women, offered their time to the Crusade, fanning out through the countryside to remote rural areas where illiteracy was highest. Even the country's bottle-tops and matchbox labels carried the message – 'Alfabetizacion es liberacion' ('literacy is liberation'). The Crusade, which ran from March to August 1980, shrank Nicaragua's illiteracy rate from 50 per cent to 12 per cent in a mere five months. Manuel's father, Donald Palacios, was one of the 400,000 Nicaraguans embracing the right to free education.

But with the outbreak of war, the school expansion was halted, and 600 schools were closed. Fifty were destroyed and 20 were damaged. In addition, 110 teachers were killed as a result of the war – murdered by guerrillas, while 70 teachers were kidnapped and an unknown number wounded. According to the World University Service:

Adult education and rural teachers, along with health and agrarian reform workers, have been a particular target for contra attack. The gains that have been made over the past nine years are now under threat, as around half of Nicaragua's annual budget has to be spent on defence against contra attack.

In 1985, all investment in education was frozen. The schools that have been developed since have been funded by international assistance.

69

After the 1979 revolution, the Sandinista government launched an educational crusade.

THE COST OF WAR

The war is not only expensive in resources but in human suffering. Sixteen thousand Nicaraguan children have had their lives shattered by the war — orphaned since the conflict with the contras began.

When a jet fell out of the sky on to the quiet Scottish town of Lockerbie, killing all the passengers and some of the townspeople, the shock waves affected not only the relatives of the dead but everyone in the area including the professional rescue workers. The British public were warned of the powerful emotional reactions people may have even months after the accident, and advised to make sure they find healthy ways to express these feelings. When 16,000 children in Nicaragua see

War with the Contras has uprooted 180,000 Nicaraguan children and left 16,000 orphaned.

their parents die violently, how much grief must they hold inside them – and who, in a war-torn country, is there to draw it out and comfort them?

Some 180,000 Nicaraguan children have had to leave their homes. Others have experienced not only emotional scars but physical injury. Because of the war, more than 1,500 children have been crippled or wounded – and nearly 500 have been assassinated. At an orthopaedic centre, children who have had their limbs amputated receive three months of treatment for their physical and their psychological traumas.

In the midst of all this, the Sandinista government struggles to teach Nicaragua's children. Under the Somoza regime, Nicaragua had the lowest education

rate in Latin America apart from Haiti. But the Sandinistas were determined to raise the level of education, whatever its other costs. At present, education remains Nicaragua's third highest priority in the national budget, after defence and industry. Says Aminta Pineda, head of the teacher training school: 'if only our situation did not require the National Budget to be directed towards defense as the first priority! With five million cordobas ($1,200) the state could maintain our school for a whole month, whereas it covers only one hour in the battlefields.'

The money left for education reflects the government's perception of educational priorities. At present the priority is to cover as many people as possible, regardless of age, and to teach them up to the fourth year of basic schooling – research on the basic minimum of education a person needs seems to point to four years' worth – rather than to educate a minority of children as far up the educational ladder as they can go. It may seem an obvious decision when a country is poor: in fact it requires a dramatic reversal of conventional spending patterns in the Third World.

Educational investment, like investment in health care, usually 'stands firmly on its apex', according to the 1989 State of the World's Children Report. 'Over 50 per cent of government spending on education in the Third World is devoted to secondary and higher education which caters to 30 per cent of the population.' As these 30 per cent usually come from the higher income groups, this means that public funds are largely being devoted to the already better off. Foreign aid for education often helps reinforce that distinction, with only 1 per cent of all aid going to primary schools.

Not only has the amount of money available for primary education been so limited, the content of the education on offer has been geared to benefit the few who go on to further study, again at the expense of the majority. 'In most cases,' the Report goes on, 'primary education is designed to prepare and select the 20–30 per cent who will go on to secondary school. It is therefore designed to fail 70–80 per cent of its intake, who then leave with an education relevant to crushed hopes rather than present realities.'

So countries like Nicaragua that are eager to democratize education must both extend its availability and improve its relevance. How is it to be done – and on a shoestring?

EDUCATION FOR ALL IN THE YEAR 2000?

The first step, as ever, must be a shift of perception: it is necessary to recognize that primary education for all should have priority over higher education

Governments spend more on secondary and further education – offered to a better-off minority – than on primary education for all.

for some. On an ethical level, it seems pretty unarguable: it is obviously ludicrous to subsidize the education of the rich while leaving the poor to finance their own. But, as we have seen, the world has not so far been run on ethical values like fairness; it tends to see a moral point only where it notices that morality makes financial sense.

A World Bank study has stated: 'World-wide experience over the past two decades demonstrates that education is a prudent economic investment, one that consistently earns high rates of return. Research also shows that returns are particularly high for educational investment in the poorest countries.'

Agricultural production, for example, among poor farmers has been found to be up to 25 per cent higher among those who have had four years of education. So, even when issues of justice are set aside, universal primary education seems a good idea. Indeed, the World Bank complains that: 'In many countries the average dollar invested in primary education returns twice as much as one invested in higher education. Yet governments in these countries heavily subsidize higher education at the expense of primary education.'

To reinforce this shift of perception, a conference on 'basic education for all' has been called, sponsored by the World Bank, UNESCO and UNICEF. The hope is that the conference will do for universal basic education what the Alma Ata conference (which promoted the notion of 'barefoot doctors') did a decade ago for primary health care – and set a target of primary education for all by the year 2000. The conference is to be held in Bangkok in March 1990.

But having agreed that universal basic education is a sound social investment in the long run, the fact remains that it has to be funded now. Funding remains a problem that a poor country has to solve.

Nearly half the world's destitute children live in India, speaking hundreds of different languages: to reach them all demands ingenuity, not conventional thinking.

MORE SCHOOLS FOR THE SAME MONEY

One tactic tried in parts of Nicaragua is operating a double-shift at school. Twice as many children can be taught in the same number of school buildings, and by the same number of teachers – if each shift is shorter and teachers are willing to work longer hours. It also means that the children of the very poor, who cannot spare a whole day for school since they must help in the fields, or perhaps sell newspapers on the streets, can still go to school. Often these children go to school in the afternoons.

The solution is not without its problems. The teachers must work long hours for little pay – 50 per cent of the teachers in Nicaragua give up, and look for better-paying jobs. And afternoon shifts are sometimes perceived by the community as providing a poorer standard of education. But research done in El Salvador (according to G. Bishop in *Innovations in Education*) indicates that the performance of students in double-session rural schools can be at least as good as that in single-session schools. And as maintaining school buildings is a heavy expense, their fuller use is welcomed. In most countries schools are closed for three months in the year and every evening. In Bahia, Brazil, school buildings are used all day, all year round.

Another, more radical form of double-shifting has been employed in rural areas of Sweden. Here, the schools have a biennial intake – that is to say, children attend school every other year between the ages of seven and thirteen, so in a six-year primary school only three classrooms and three teachers are needed. Apparently, 'this stratagem pays off almost as much as if they had six years of full-time schooling,' though this may partly be because Swedish children live in a society affluent enough for learning to be maintained informally out of school.

A heartfelt complaint made by a group of poor children from Italian peasant families was that they hated the 'unfairness' of breaks from school. During the school holidays, they said, the middle-class schoolchildren continued to learn: the culture of their family life reinforced their school-learning through books, theatre-trips, travel, stimulating conversation . . . But they, in their peasant families, were condemned to lonely weeks where illiterate parents worked exhausting hours and had neither time for talking nor money for theatre-going, and the children forgot what they had learned in term-time.

Multi-grade teaching is yet another response to keeping down costs. If a village community cannot afford a teacher and a classroom for each year-group, children of different ages are taught together. Sometimes this is called 'family grouping', since these groups resemble families who rarely have children all of one age. In Britain this idea was fashionable in educational circles in the 1960s; some small schools, threatened with closure as 'uneconomic', adopted this policy and found they enjoyed it. Often, older children in the group would naturally help the younger ones, and this community-spirited, non-competitive behaviour was recognized as an added benefit for all the children. Sometimes – in Cuba, for instance – this help was formalized into a monitorial system where older pupils regularly taught younger ones.

Other countries have experimented with other ways to overturn the top-heavy educational triangle. When both South Korea and Taiwan decided to invest heavily in primary education in the 1960s, the free primary schooling they offered everywhere was financed in part by charges for secondary and tertiary education – a less than ideal solution, since it means that only those who can afford to can go on to post-primary school. Yet another approach has been tried in China and Cuba, where the governments strictly limit the number of students who get more than ten years' schooling to those for whom jobs requiring such higher education were available.

Clearly, poor countries go to great lengths to offer their children whatever formal education they can. Education is something the poor believe in – sometimes more than those who have had a lot of it.

But why should education make such a difference? UNICEF's James Grant explains that: 'Education enhances the investments made in almost every other aspect of the development effort. The cost–benefit ratio has changed but through an increase in perceived benefit rather than a reduction in per capita cost.'

To put it very simply, if we were to calculate that it cost $50 to offer primary education to a child, and then we calculated that this child earned the country $60 more as a result of this education than he otherwise would have, we would probably consider our investment worthwhile. But if we were to discover later that the child's education also saved us a further $90 in other, unexpected ways, then we would be delighted with our investment. We would still have spent the same 'per capita cost' of $50, but we will now perceive the 'cost–benefit ratio' differently.

This is exactly what has been happening, as in the example provided by the farmers. The increased agricultural production was an unexpected bonus. But perhaps the most startling change in 'perceived benefit' came with the realization that, by educating girls, a country could save itself thousands of infant lives. It seems, astonishingly, that the education of girls is the *biggest single factor in the drop in infant mortality rates.*

WHY TEACHING GIRLS IS A PRIORITY

Development writer Peter Adamson reported this finding on the effects of educating girls thus:

In the mid-1970s, Professor Iram Orubuloye and Professor John Caldwell completed a remarkable piece of research in two villages of Eastern Nigeria. The object of their study was to see if public health services reduced infant deaths.

In one of the villages, clinics were conveniently located and frequently used. In the other, there were no public health services within manageable distance. Apart from this one significant difference, the two villages were

Educating girls may be more important, not less, than educating boys.

Adamson discovered that surveys in at least 25 different nations had come to the conclusion that child health improves with the level of the mother's education. But the assumption underlying these surveys had been that if a mother was more educated, then she must be better off – and that this higher social and economic status was what gave her child a better chance. The Nigerian study by Orubuloye and Caldwell overturned this assumption. It seemed that 'the mother's level of education was a powerful lever *in its own right* for raising the level of child health' (Adamson).

Professor Caldwell, after many years of research, is unequivocal:

Maternal education is the single most significant determinant of these marked differences in child mortality. Such differences are also affected by a large range of other socio-economic factors but *no other factor has the impact of maternal education.*

Both Adamson and Caldwell believe that the reason for education exerting such a powerful influence is a psychological one. Says Adamson, 'Education undermines fatalism and resignation, substituting a degree of confidence, a different perception of the possible . . . a belief that decisions can be made, circumstances changed, lives improved.'

Caldwell shows how the mother's sense of empowerment changes the family circle:

The education of the woman greatly changes the traditional balance of familial relationships with profound effects on child care . . . A woman with schooling is more likely to challenge her mother-in-law and the mother-in-law is much less likely to fight the challenge. The younger women will assert the wisdom of the school against the wisdom of the old. She is more likely to attempt to communicate with her husband, and her husband is less likely to reject the attempt.

But how does this heightened maternal confidence stop babies dying? One suggestion is that the confident, educated woman, who is listened to

broadly similar in levels of food supply and access to water and sanitation. The results showed that the use of public health clinics did indeed reduce the rate of infant deaths. But it also showed something less obvious.

In the 'healthy' village, a baby born to an illiterate woman was found to be two-and-a-half times more likely to die in childhood than a baby born to a mother who had been to school. When the data from the village without health services was examined, the effect of the mother's education was seen to be even more pronounced. There, the child of an educated woman was found to be *four* times more likely to survive.

with more respect by her husband, may be able to persuade him to use contraception rather than require her to spend her life in childbirth. The smaller, better-spaced family that the mother prefers is also healthier for her babies. As we saw in chapter 3, birth-spacing improves the chances of the babies' survival.

This has a further repercussion: parents who feel confident their babies will survive are happy to have fewer children – they don't need to have many to ensure that one or two will survive as 'insurance' for their old age. The small, healthy family that is now created is easier for the family – and for the nation – to feed and educate well. And the better the children are fed and educated, the more likely they, in turn, are to have babies that survive . . . A benign cycle has been set in motion.

But is this the only way in which the empowerment of the mother makes a difference to her baby's health and survival? Research in the North has been producing fascinating glimpses into the complex and subtle relationship between a parent and a baby: for example, how a happy, confident mother (unlike an anxious, preoccupied one with low self-esteem) will intuitively mirror the baby back to himself – and how this is a crucial requirement for the child's healthy development. How long will it

Educate a girl and you educate a nation.

be before more psychological research is applied to parents and children in the poor world? It is dismaying that the careful consideration of what goes on inside people's minds and hearts is generally reserved for the affluent while the poor usually have to make do with statistics about their bodies.

Whatever the reasons turn out to be, the education of the mother does seem to have a mysteriously powerful impact on infant mortality. So education is valuable not only for the girls that are empowered but for succeeding generations. As someone once said, 'Educate a boy and you will educate a person. Educate a girl and you will educate a nation.'

But are girls being educated?

DEBT STRIKES AT SCHOOLGIRLS

In 1960, the average rate of female school enrolment in the poorer half of the world was only just over 30 per cent. By 1986, it was more than 80 per cent. In China, nearly 100 per cent of girls attended primary schools, while the rate of enrolment had doubled, or almost doubled, in Bangladesh, Nepal, Somalia, Zaire, Mozambique, Tanzania, Sudan, Ghana, Kenya, Zambia, Papua New Guinea, Morocco, Tunisia, Syria, Algeria, Iran, Iraq, Libya . . .

But once again a note of caution must be struck – in fact, two notes. One is that girls who enrol don't always stay on at school: the demands of the family suck them back home, where they service the needs of the family circle at the expense of their own. And the second is that the burden of debt repayments keeps growing. In the same way that the daughters sacrifice their own needs to service the family, the poorer nations service the demands of the global marketplace at the expense of their people's needs. Until this debt burden is lifted, countries will be hampered in their efforts to improve the national economy; and while the resulting economic decline keeps poor people poor, girls will tend to get left out of school. And that will not only keep half the next generation disempowered but will also keep up the population rate and the infant death rate. The debt burden obstructs the potentially benign cycle set in motion by education.

In the past 40 years, the absolute number of children in the Third World has doubled. None the less, the poor countries' commitment to education has been such that the proportion of children in school has not halved – amazingly enough, it has *doubled*: that makes a four-fold increase in the educational services offered. 'Such enrolment figures represent one of the developing world's greatest achievements,' says the State of the World's Children Report. 'In 1986, the percentage of six- to 11-year-old boys and girls in primary schools was approximately 100% and 99% respectively in Latin America; 69% and 45% in South Asia; and 80% and 65% in Africa.'

But in the past few years, the improvement has been slowing down or even reversing as a direct result of the debt burden and economic recession. As many as 50 per cent of children may drop out, and even enrolment rates are falling. The Report continues:

On present trends, it seems likely that the children of the poorest 15–20% of families are going to be excluded from literacy for decades to come. It would be a tragedy if that were allowed to happen – if the spread of education were to stop short after coming so far. One of the greatest challenges for development in the next twenty years is going to be [reaching] the very poorest groups and creating the conditions in which they can improve their own lives.

But in as many as half of the developing nations, spending per pupil has declined in the 1980s.

IRRELEVANT EDUCATION

So far we have focused on the quantity of education available to children in the poor world but not its relevance. And by 'education', so far, we have meant the sort of instruction that we are accustomed to receiving in institutional buildings known as schools, dispensed by authority figures known as teachers, in classrooms where children sit obediently in rows. But even if the Third World could ever afford enough classrooms and teachers like this, is this the sort of education we want for our children? 'Parishar Asha' is an Environmental Education Centre in India. Its director, Gloria de Souza, denounces conventional education as 'a de-humanizing system' that is a 'form of child abuse'. She quotes Einstein:

It is nothing short of a miracle that our methods of instruction have not yet entirely strangled the holy curiosity of enquiry: for this delicate plant, aside from stimulation, stands mainly in need of freedom. Without this, it goes to wrack and ruin.

In Bombay, she says, teacher–pupil ratios are 1:65, making personalized teaching virtually impossible. The children learn – if 'learn' is the right word – through 'a rote-learning system where memory serves as a crutch for non-comprehension'. It is hardly surprising that children are taught in this way, she adds, since 'most Indian teachers are themselves products of a rote-learning system, with little or no exposure to creative problem-solving'. Further, English is increasingly the language of schools even though the children's first language is not English.

English is the language of the middle class – and of India's colonizers. And learning through the medium of a language that clearly belongs to a group which is not your own, but which has power over you, is a well-known way to continue the pattern of disempowerment. In Sri Lanka before independence from the British in 1947, children were sometimes fined for each word they spoke at school in their own language, Sinhala. It was a potent way to convey the message that the language of the colonial masters was the 'right' language and the child's own language 'wrong' – and, by implication, that the colonizers' culture, mirrored in

What are schools for – training, social filtering, or developing a child's sense of meaning?

the language, was superior to that of the child's ancestors.

In Soweto, the schoolchildren's riots in the 1970s were triggered off by the South African government's attempt to impose Afrikaans at school. Language is a key part of a child's identity: children know how important it is to choose a language of instruction that gives force to their own identity, rather than to someone else's.

'What is most frustrating,' de Souza concludes, 'is an almost de-sensitized acceptance on the part of most teachers, parents, and even some decision-makers, that one cannot expect schools and colleges to be more than a formal channel for obtaining certificates as passports' – that is, passports into jobs. Education like this has little to do with offering a child any information or skill of relevance to his life. It is more a means of acquiring a piece of paper that certifies a child's acceptability to one authority in order to be accepted by another – a tool of social control.

This kind of education does not attempt to respond to the child's wonder at the extraordinary planet he lives on, and at what an extraordinary being he himself is, or to puzzle over the relationship of the one to the other. The yearning to understand how and why life works as it does is not alien to children. Meaning and purpose matter: the nature of reality beckons. Every parent knows that if they spend quiet, unpressured time alone with their children, the questions that arise are ageless and profound: 'Why are we born? What exists after the end of the universe? Why is there so much trouble in the world? I am like a different person when I am with different people – who am I really? Do I see the colour you see? How do we ever know what another person really sees? What should I do in my life?'

These questions are vital to children. And the fact that they keep asking them is more important than getting fixed answers to them, for these are the sorts of questions, asked constantly, that keep minds and hearts awake. They are not the sort of questions there is room to ponder on in most schools.

But they are asked in two sorts of innovative schools which we will go on to look at in some detail – one found in a community that is among the richest in the world, and the other among the poorest.

COMMUNITIES OF LEARNING

The first of these schools are to be found in Denmark, where the students at the *folkehojskoler* – or 'people's colleges' – are encouraged to ask fundamental questions. As Peter de la Cour writes in *Danish Model:*

There is no rigidly laid down curriculum at the people's colleges. Not only that, but in recognition of the dangerous tendency of most teachers to equate education with certification, the people's colleges are by law prevented from doing any examinations-oriented work.... The educational process is given priority over content.... *[They] are communities of learning, not teaching.*

A famous nineteenth century Danish principal of a people's college put it like this, 'The aim of the people's college is to be defined by the area in which the yearnings

of the students meet with the talents of the teachers.' The emphasis is on creating a community of near-equals, where the teachers are merely *primus inter pares.* Hence good teachers . . . are primarily facilitators and catalysts and have relinquished much of the authority traditionally associated with the teachers' role. It is an important part of the tradition that students – who significantly are always referred to as course participants rather than as students – should be empowered to play an important part in most aspects of the life of the college.

So students and staff prepare food, eat, clean, engage in sport and musical activities, and sort out the practicalities of college life together. The course participants are not small children, however. They are at least 17. But even in respect of schools catering for pupils up to 16, the *folkeskolen,* Danish law states that:

Folkeskolen should prepare pupils for participation and co-determination of our democratic society in order that they can assume co-responsibility for seeking solutions to common problems. Freedom of expression, intellectual liberty and democracy must therefore be the foundations upon which the schools' existence is built . . . The planning and detailed arrangements relating to all educational matters, including the choice of curricular content, teaching methods and organizational structure, *must be decided jointly by the teachers and the pupils.* (My italics)

In the Danish 'people's colleges' (folkehojskoler), pupils play an active and democratic role in deciding the curriculum.

This is a far cry from the reality in most schools in the world, where school staff equate a child's 'responsible behaviour' with obedience: the idea of a child learning in partnership with teachers would be abhorrent. As one British headmaster of a private school said, 'There are only two rules in this school, always to tell the truth and always to do as you are told.' He seems not to have noticed – or assumes the children won't – that the second rule encompasses any rule he may care to dream up.

Indeed, for the majority of schoolchildren, school may not seem a place that exists for their development: it is there to confirm society's expectation of them as failures. A young teacher working in Oxford described to me how she was given the 'drop-out' group to teach as part of her first job. These 15–16-year-olds were due to leave school as soon as they were legally allowed to at the end of the academic year, after sitting a national exam. No one in the school, staff or pupils, expected them to pass the exam: it was just a formality to prove the pupils' failure. (That's why they were given the youngest, least experienced teacher – there was no point 'wasting' a better teacher on this group.)

But the young teacher hadn't yet learned the rules of the school game. She was idealistic enough to imagine that the school was a place where children were meant to be educated and empowered. In her naïvety, she threw herself into helping the children overcome their low self-esteem. An exhausting, depressing, exhilarating year later, when the children sat the national exam, they passed with flying colours. One child was awarded a distinction. The children were astounded, and as proud of themselves as the teacher was of them.

And the reaction of the other staff? A single chilling remark: 'Oh no. Now they'll want to stay on and lower the tone of the senior school.'

Society has fixed ideas about the colour, class, gender and numbers of the children it expects to do well. It does not take kindly to these fixed ideas being overturned. A famous study once showed that white children who spoke up in class were considered 'bright' by their teachers and rewarded – while black children who spoke up were considered 'uppity' and punished. Girls have had the same experience.

EMPTY VESSELS

In addition to the financial difficulties, then, of finding enough classrooms and teachers to educate children, we have to ask a question that relates to our values: do adults want children to be empowered at school? Do we genuinely want teachers who draw out the children before them – or do we actually prefer teachers who mould the children into shapes that won't challenge the adults in charge?

One headteacher was emphatic that adults should mould children like clay pots, one hand inside the pot and one outside. Doesn't this assume a child is an empty vessel? What about the child's own personality, needs, emotions? The headteacher withdrew from such ideas almost with a shudder. 'Being interested in oneself,' he said firmly, 'makes one a weak man.'

Not every educator is this terrified to look at himself. Others, like the distinguished Third World educator Soedjatmoko, former Rector of the UN University, argue that the world is changing so fast that just training children is pointless – real education must be about children understanding themselves and other people in the world they live in. It does seem short-sighted to assume that children who are empowered to understand themselves must be weak and egoistic, when the opposite seems nearer the truth. Surely the egoist is the one who doesn't examine himself, because he thinks he is perfectly fine as he is. Soedjatmoko also believes that the new schooling must encompass everyone in society, including the dispossessed and destitute, if the world is to move towards peace and justice for all.

Perhaps the best-known of the Third World educationalists, Ivan Illich and Paulo Freire, believe that the sort of education that genuinely empowers

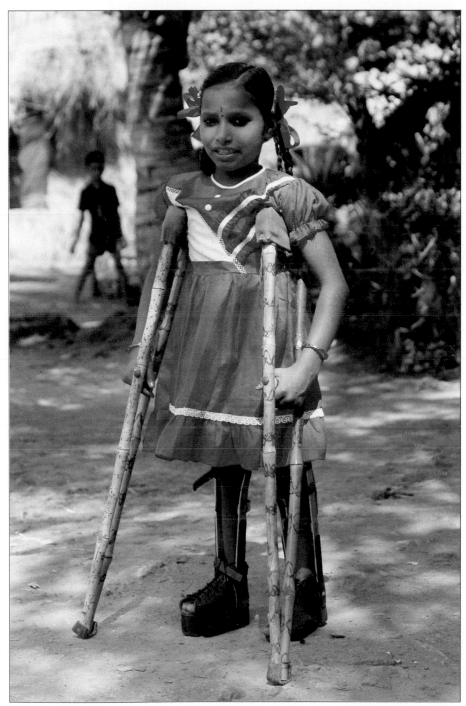

Gopamma missed being immunized – and caught Polio when she was two.

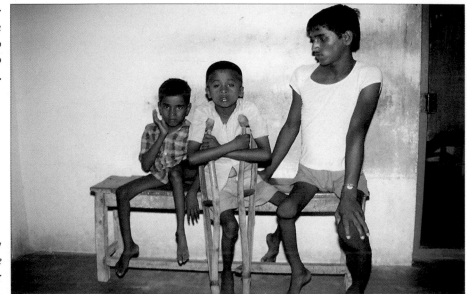

Every year another 200,000 children in India are added to the list of polio victims.

Gopamma's family still depends on the contaminated water that gave her polio.

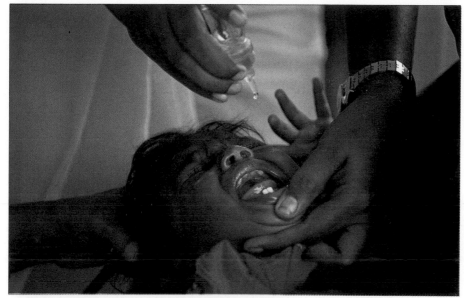

A child receiving polio vaccine. The incidence of polio has been reduced by 25 per cent in the 1980s – and, says UNICEF, could be eradicated worldwide by the year 2000.

A mother visits her child at the Arthwick Samata Mandel Hospital – where Gopamma too was helped to regain the use of her legs

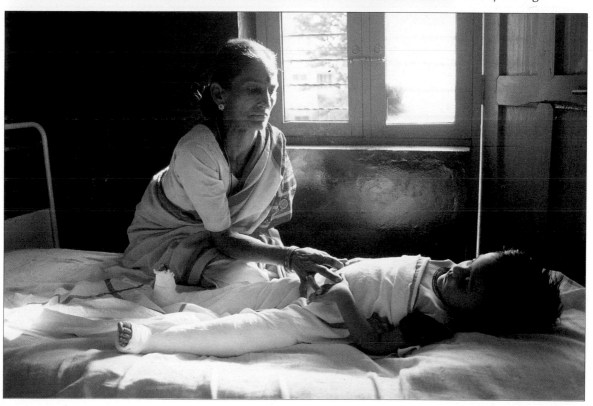

Africa: a malnourished child is more susceptible to diseases that can lead to disablement or death.

Development has been concentrated in the cities, many of which are ringed by burgeoning slums.

Overuse of the land for grazing and cash crops has exacerbated the spread of deserts.

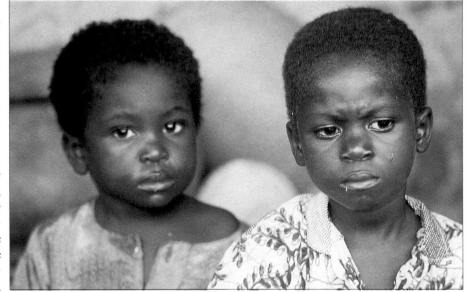

Mary Nti and her son. Immunized as well as breastfed, her parents have got him off to the best start in life they can provide.

At home in the village of Ntinanko, these children have caring parents – but their future depends on market forces beyond their parents' control.

Clean water is a must for child health. Diarrhoeal diseases are the biggest killer of children under five.

Cocoa pods are Ghana's life-line. When the price of cocoa falls on the commodity markets, Ghana's children go hungry.

As dept repayments bite into government budgets, even basic health programmes for children are cut back.

Nicaragua: 16,000 children have been orphaned in Nicaragua since the Contra war began. Who will comfort all these children?

Children in Nicaragua have learned to live – and even to play – in the inhuman shadow of war.

The year 2000 has been targeted as the date by which every child should have the chance to go to school.

To educate a girl is – surprisingly – to give her future babies a better chance of survival.

Children in rural Nicaragua sometimes go to double shift schools – so they can work in the fields for half the day.

*What can education
do for a child – train
him for a job that
doesn't exist, or give
him a sense of
purpose in life?*

*Poor communities
can't wait until they
have desks and
chairs for their
children – they start
the process of
learning with
whatever they can
improvise.*

individuals also empowers the community. They argue that education should be related to the felt needs of the people who are doing the learning – to their daily needs and their political needs as citizens of a democratic state. 'Conscientized' was the word Freire popularized, and despite its awkwardness it has become indispensable in global educational discussions.

Illich wanted to 'de-school' society, replacing schools with 'skill centres', where anyone in the community, at any stage of his or her life, could come and learn – or come and teach. Schooling was to be a lifelong affair, from cradle to grave, and open to everyone with a talent to offer, not something to be monopolized by a group of teachers lording it over the young for a fixed period.

In *The Pedagogy of the Oppressed*, a book whose content is as opaque as its title, Freire made a crucial point: people who are oppressed tend to 'internalize' an image of their oppressor. Most of us have shared this experience of an internalized oppressor. Which of us has not heard a voice in our heads persistently doubting and criticizing us? In this way, says Freire, the oppressed are divided against themselves: one part of them wants to be confident, independent and free but is undermined by another part which sees them through the eyes of the oppressor and judges them as only good enough to obey the master. Until the oppressed victim stops victimizing himself like this, he will never be free of the thrall of the oppressor.

The process of internalizing the oppressor recalls what we saw happening between pimps and child prostitutes (see chapter 2), when the child takes into herself the pimp's opinion of her (she is bad and deserves to be punished) while giving away to him her good qualities (he is good and deserves care). Indeed, it happens in any relationship where there is a power imbalance that is misused – for example, in schools where passive children are obliged to swallow teachers' opinions about everything, including themselves. Education must go beyond treating children as empty vessels waiting to be filled. Children have a right to education which treats them as *actors* who have something of their own to express. Some centuries ago, when a young artist went to paint the ceiling of the Sistine Chapel, he was accompanied by a note which read: 'The bearer of these presents is the sculptor Michelangelo. His nature is such that he needs to be drawn out by kindness and encouragement, but if love be shown him and he be treated kindly, he will accomplish things that will make the whole world wonder.' There are some schools which do draw out the creative, expressive qualities even of the poorest children – like the schools founded by Pedro Orata in the Philippines, the second type of innovative school at which we will look in some detail.

DO-IT-YOURSELF SCHOOLS

Dr Pedro T. Orata is a winner of the Ramon Magsaysay Award, a Third World equivalent of the Nobel Prize awarded to Asians who have made an outstanding contribution to public service. He is the founder of the Barrio Village Education Movement in the Philippines (a *barrio* is a neighbourhood). By the mid-1980s, the movement had educated a quarter of a million pupils who would otherwise have had virtually no education at all. Instead their education has been enviable – relevant to their individual lives as well as useful to their communities. Says Dr Orata:

If we had waited until all was well provided – buildings, textbooks, science equipment, well qualified teachers, the 250,000 children and young people who are now enrolled in some 1,500 barrio high schools, forty-five community colleges and 500 pre-schools would still be waiting for a chance to go to school.

So where did all the buildings, equipment and teachers come from?

We started from where people were, with what they had, with existing school facilities, equipment and personnel, and proceeded one step forward – or even half a step – at

Children from the barrio schools in the Philippines.

a time, the people themselves (children and adults) helping to make the decisions, formulate the plans, carry them out and assess their performance, on the basis of which they helped revise the programme.

The only way to start is to start, and the place to start is right here with what little we have – and with even a negative quantity. We did not wait for experts to come, or for money to be appropriated, or for certain things to be done for us. Had we waited, we would still be waiting. Our only capital was ourselves, our health, our determination to succeed, and of course our own resources – land, artesian wells, canals and some shovels, and good humour. We did not have any budget. We studied our needs, made plans, and went ahead as best we could.

The purpose of this positive approach was to avoid the all too common practice in the Philippines: of starting with a recital of a long list of problems and difficulties, after which everybody is discouraged and no one dares make a start. We started by doing things that were possible with existing facilities and personnel. . . . Once simple projects have been undertaken successfully, the more difficult ones are more easily handled.

The children building up the barrio schools in this way avoided falling into the trap of seeing themselves as helpless victims, dependent on someone powerful to pick them up – and seeing powerful people as necessarily other people, never themselves. They started to depend on their own power and to recognize, therefore, that they did have power within themselves. The first step in self-empowerment is recognition – recognition that although other people may have more obvious access to certain kinds of strengths, like money or influence, we all have some strengths; our chief bar to our own strength is the assumption that we have none. And this experience of autonomy is the seed-bed for a child's sense that she is entitled to rights of her own.

In this way the barrio schools not only honoured the child's right to receive an education, a developmental right given her by society, but helped to uncover that sense of an intrinsic 'right to rights' before a single formal lesson had been taught.

And what about the tangible necessities of school life? The children improvised equipment. By recycling cast-off objects like burned out light bulbs, empty cans and bottles, worn out tyres, corn husks, bits of bamboo and wood, they made science equipment for the older children and play equipment for pre-schoolers. And when the pupils discovered a scientific principle, they put it into practice; for example, when they learned about irrigation, they laid out a bamboo irrigation system.

Also, they shared what they knew with their classmates – and with their neighbours. So not only did the children and their teachers get the intellectual benefit of flexing and developing their creativity and problem-solving ability, but the community benefited directly from the school's learning.

School, then, was no longer the starting point of a rat-race, an institution where children swot and sweat so they can scramble into the few academic places available and wave a relieved goodbye to their intellectually 'inferior' friends; it was about developing every child's creative ability, and helping them to express that talent in ways that benefited

both themselves and their neighbours. It was about self-worth, and about making a genuine contribution to the community to which they belonged. The barrio school in this way became a community centre, not cut off from the mainstream of life.

There was an interesting by-product of these barrio schools. A local authority totted up the amount of juvenile crime in the disadvantaged area where the schools were operating and came to a startling conclusion: in one year, in the three barrios where the home-made schools had been set up, not a single crime had been committed by young people. What had happened to the habitual violence? It seemed to have disappeared along with the despair.

So once again the 'cost–benefit' of real education could be perceived differently. It could be set against the high cost of crime and crime prevention. And the advantages conferred by the barrio schools were not merely social and psychological. The children in these do-it-yourself schools generally achieved more academically than pupils in the corresponding high schools.

THE NEW TEACHER

Dr Orata is uncompromising about the nature of the relationship that must exist between the barrio school movement facilitators and the local community. Whatever leadership they offer must come not from an attitude of patronage but from its polar opposite: solidarity.

We tried, in every situation, to live by the principle that a good leader must be a good follower. There is not a single activity in which we, the leaders, acted in the capacity of overseers. When there was digging to do, we had our own shovels and used them . . . The leader must live [in the community] and with their problems.

The famous put-down about teachers is that 'those who can, do; those who can't, teach'. Although unfair to some teachers, this generalization reflects the popular perception that teachers are adults who liked the cocooned atmosphere of schools when

The traditional role of the teacher is under threat: will teachers take the chance to become community leaders?

The teacher will no longer lead a double life, shutting himself up in his school to teach children and only emerging to lose himself within an anonymous mass of citizens. His role does not stop at the school gate. Outside school and after school, he is still a teacher; within school, during school hours, he is already a community leader.

The Third World's innovatory educators like Orata exemplify the new-look teacher.

State-aided schools or very cheap community schools like Orata's are needed if children are to have equal educational opportunities. The danger in state-funded education is that authorities can insist on a 'National Curriculum' (like that being introduced now in Britain), so that the children and their parents have no say in what the pupils spend most of their day learning. The child's right to education becomes converted into *the child's obligation to learn what the state decides it has a right to teach*.

Is this the state caring for the child's best interests — or is the child being used to look after the interests of the state? Adding insult to injury, privately funded schools (to which most members of the British government send their own children) are excluded from this obligation — on the specious ground that 'freedom' is a virtue that must be vigilantly maintained. Apparently the freedom of the child in a state-funded school is of no consequence.

I put the point to a government minister from Jamaica in the old Seaga administration. 'And why shouldn't the state tell people what to learn?' she said angrily. 'If the state has paid for their education, they should expect to do what they're told.'

The barrio village schools appear to be free of this kind of pressure, which is disturbingly reminiscent of Huxley's nightmarish 'Brave New World' where a few children are creamed off to become rulers while the rest are obliged 'to do what they are told'. 'The philosophy of the barrio high schools,' says Orata, 'is to give every Filipino the opportunity to develop his capacities to the utmost. This right is as important as the right to life and food.'

they were children, and have now devised a way to get back in there. The main characteristic of this kind of teacher is, indeed, his disconnection with the 'real' outside world.

But this kind of teacher has little place in the new education, where teachers need to be men and women who are in the mainstream of life. They are described well in *An Experiment in the Ruralization of Education* by R. Lallez:

Clearly, he is not talking about the child's right to be trained in a few technical skills, like reading or adding up; he is talking about the child's right to become a fully empowered human being. Innovatory schools like this – and the other innovatory ideas from the Third World, a very few of which have been touched on in this chapter – must be looked at by policy-makers before they decide that it is too expensive to educate all the children of the world.

It may be that the schoolchildren of the future will be able to by-pass centuries of irrelevant education – and jump straight into schooling that recognizes the importance of empowerment, both for the sake of children as individuals and for the sake of the communities in which they live.

6

THE DEVIL
MAKES WORK

Of course children are a source of cheap labour. That is as it should be. What spoiled little brats they would be if they were a source of expensive labour.

Keith Waterhouse, Daily Mirror

Italy has pensioners, partial invalids for the rest of their lives, aged 13.

Letizia is one of them. When her father lost his job, 13-year-old Letizia went to work in a small workshop, making shoes. She sat on the glueing bench for ten hours a day, the smell of the glue very strong in a room that held 22 other workers. Soon Letizia began to have trouble with her eyes and to suffer stomach pains, and then a skin complaint on her hands. Within three months of starting to work, she lost weight, felt constant nausea and a sharp tingling in her arms and legs.

One day, without warning, she fell down and could not get up again. She was taken to hospital – and later discharged as fit, although her legs remained paralysed. Three months later, she was taken to hospital again, and this time she was kept in for five months. Even her arms were almost completely paralysed, so she couldn't feed herself. This time when she returned home, she was just able to walk with a support and, very slowly and with much effort, to feed herself.

Letizia's condition, says Marina Valcarenghi in her report on child labour in Italy for the Anti-Slavery Society, has never improved: she drags herself around, she falls easily, drops things and cannot walk without support.

Another child, Francesca, aged 14, describes what it was like to work in one of these small shoe factories:

Winter was approaching and the window by our section was closed. . . . The place where twenty-five of us worked was 10 metres [long]. Because a large number of [us] were working in such a constricted area, we had to sit with our backs against each other. The air became unbreatheable because of the stench that could not escape through the single window. The whole place was damp and unhealthy; there were spiders, cockroaches and rats. Our cloakroom was a tiny room in which the gum and solvents were also stored. After work, when we went to get changed, we would find our clothes damp, cold and reeking of gum.

Within months, Francesca, too, was as ill as Letizia.

To start with I felt sick and went off my food; then I began to notice a tingling in my ankles, knees and arms. I had no idea what caused this and went on working till I had not the strength to get up. By March I could no longer walk. A buckling of the legs caused me several times to fall to the ground at work.

Francesca spent time in and out of hospital – where the treatment given was perfunctory and failed to restore the child to health. 'After twenty days, I was discharged as my bed was needed. The doctor said that physiotherapy as an out-patient would be quite sufficient.' So, three times a week, she must make her slow and painful way to hospital; and since she cannot walk alone, her mother must also take time away from her work to accompany her. All this underlines the inadequate care offered her at the hospital when she gets there; the electric shock treatment, for instance, which exacerbates her already nervous, debilitated state.

Neither at the workplace nor at the hospital is the community taking due care of these young girls; it seems that they are being treated as commodities to be exploited as long as they can be useful, and then cast away perfunctorily like spent batteries when their energies are used up. The community does not grieve over the childhood it has stolen – nor the potential adulthood it has wasted: on the contrary, it will not 'waste' more than a face-saving minimum of its energy on these sad, ruined children.

Francesca says:

I often think about my situation and that of so many other companions who have to suffer such isolation. We do not know when all this will be over. One of our work companions was expecting a baby which was born paralysed.

Even if I recover, the functioning of my muscles will always be below normal. I no longer have a job. They dismissed me as soon as I was awarded my disability pension.

HOMEWORK – BUT NOT FOR THE TEACHER

These teenage pensioners are just two of the million-and-a-half children estimated to be working in Italy. The worst areas are Naples, Milan, Turin, Genoa and the provinces of Apulia, Sicily and Alazio. The Italian Trades Union Congress estimates that 100,000 children work in the Naples region alone, where 64 per cent of the children play truant from school. And 200,000 children work in Sicily,

Thousands of Italian children work in small factories instead of going to school.

where two out of five 14-year-olds play truant. What do they do instead of going to school?

Many work in small factories or workshops like Letizia and Francesca. Others are 'homeworkers' or 'outworkers', even smaller cogs in a system where piece-work is farmed out to be done in homes. Both these kinds of work have been increasing as industrialists have become eager to decentralize production – though their idea of 'decentralization' isn't what reformers like Gandhi meant by the term.

Gandhi advocated decentralized village industries run cooperatively by villages for their own benefit (for example, he encouraged villagers to spin and weave their own cotton cloth) so that they would become self-sufficient; he wanted the poor not to be dependent on working in large mills and factories owned by the rich, where they were exploited. But the decentralization in Italy isn't about the diffusion of independence and power. On the contrary, the workshops and the outworkers are the last links in a long chain of exploitation. The goods that these workers produce so cheaply are not for their use: they are exported to other parts of the country or even other parts of the world. All along the journey between shoe-maker and customer, middlemen take their cut: and in order that their cuts should be as big as possible, the workers who make the shoes are paid as little as possible.

If these workers did their jobs in a large factory, their poor working conditions might be exposed by state inspectors. Outworking not only saves the industrialist the risk of being inspected, it also saves him overheads. Often he doesn't even have to pay for the machinery used – the outworker supplies and maintains her own machine. A further advantage of outworking to the industrialist is that it discourages unionization – and, divided, the outworkers fall. All this is true of hiring outworkers of any age. Hiring children underlines the advantages to the employers: children dare to complain about conditions less often than their fathers, they get pregnant less often than their mothers, and they aren't old enough to join unions. And they can be paid even less: where an adult homeworker is paid 350 lire per pair of shoes, a child is paid 50 lire.

Children are doing the work of adults, while being paid as children. Judge Michele Di Lecce of the Labour Division of the Milan Magistrates' Court confirms that:

Anyone who uses child labour . . . is nearly always someone on the edge of the production process. . . . For small enterprises to be remunerative, they must be able to pass on part of the exploitation (to which they themselves are subjected) to their own workers. This takes the form of exacting shiftwork, minimum safety conditions, and also child labour which obviously costs less.

So child labour shows up, in exaggerated form, a labour problem woven deeply into the fabric of an unequal society. Where adult workers are vulnerable to exploitation by the powerful, there too will children be exploited, and to an even greater degree.

THE STATE AS PROTECTOR

But Italy has laws against child labour. Can't these be invoked? In theory, yes – but who will invoke them? The understaffed, apathetic inspectorate makes little impact. It is almost impossible for the inspectorate to keep track of conditions in thousands of small, scattered workplaces. Even when an inspector does go through the legal processes to close down a workshop, he knows it will simply be moved and set up again under another name a few

The state forbids child labour, but parents collude with employers to send children to work.

days later. The frustrated inspectors see their job as little more than a pointless game. 'No one doing this type of work feels motivated,' is the frank assessment of Dr Emilia Capelli Caimi, Guardianship Judge at the Milan Juvenile Court. 'If anyone does move and act on his own initiative he is considered mad rather than efficient.'

Does anyone stand fiercely on the side of the working children? It is far easier to find people ready to exploit them. The most sinister form of this exploitation system manifests in the interest taken by the Mafia, or Mafia-style organizations, in child labour. Marina Valcarenghi believes that these have penetrated the labour market in Milan as well as in Sicily, and they spread a cloak of silence over the working children: 'Every child interviewed, always after much difficulty, refused to name his employer.' At Cinisello Balsamo, in the industrial belt of Milan, Valcarenghi was twice stopped and warned not to continue 'since, so it was made plain, child labour did not exist'.

The Mafia first forces employers to use child labour – and then uses the fact of the employer's illegal use of children to blackmail him into continuing the practice. So, paradoxically, the illegality of child labour is used to promote rather than to prevent children being employed. The more that age limits are fixed and restrictions imposed, ironically, the greater is the spread of clandestine child labour.

But if the state is against child labour and employers have sometimes to be coaxed to take more children on, where do all these hundreds of thousands of children appear from, wanting jobs? It could only happen if parents supplied their children for employment – and that is exactly what happens.

Far from standing between a child and the employer, parents are often grateful to an employer who gives a child a job. Some will collude with the employer to keep the child working even when the child is desperately unhappy at work. In 1976 Michele Colonna, an Italian shepherd boy aged 14, committed suicide. Sold at the age of ten to a farmer, he lived a life of virtual slavery, getting up at 3 a.m. to look after his master's 200 sheep. Michele ran away several times but his father always sent him back.

Finally he could stand it no more and he shot himself. Public opinion was temporarily outraged, according to *All Work and No Play* (a joint publication by UNICEF and the British TUC): 'But today, travelling in Southern Italy and Sardinia, you can still see little shepherd boys like Michele roaming the mountain slopes from dawn to dusk with their flocks.'

Magistrates complain that they can't enforce child labour laws when they are dealing with a conspiracy of silence that involves members of the family, as well as the employers – and sometimes even the child workers themselves: 'No one speaks up, no one informs and we cannot take any action.' When an accident occurs that requires hospital treatment, excuses are made like 'I burnt myself at the fireplace,' 'a stone fell on my finger'.

The attitude of conspiracy to maintain child labour has soaked into the culture. Child labour is often not seen as a stain, a pollutant, but as a normal part of society. It is those who try to stop it that are seen as dubious. Says a magistrate, Dr Giovanni Vacca:

Anyone who reports to the police or the courts is an 'informer'. This fear of informing and of the consequent disapproval of the community and the family also acts as an obstacle to the most elementary solidarity amongst workers. For instance, a few days ago a worker came to report an offence... He hesitated a long time before coming to see me and his greatest concern was that his identity should not be known.

A report on industrial accidents among child labourers (*Infortuni Sul Lavoro dei Minori* by Berlinguer, Cecchini and Terranova) confirms that 'Child labour is a recurrent feature of Italian history. ... It has never represented an anomaly, a pathological excrescence, easy to remove from a healthy body, but has on the contrary been a component of the basic malformation of family life.'

THE FAMILY ENERGY SUPPLY

But in response to what obstacle has this 'malformation' arisen? Many poorer parents see sending their child out to work as their best means of fulfilling their parental responsibilities: children need to be supervised and their energies productively used – and if children don't go to work, what are they going to do all day while their parents are working? The devil makes work for idle hands, say the parents. Children on the streets 'get into bad company' or risk traffic accidents or the attentions of drug peddlers; much better that they should learn a trade to keep them in good stead when they are older. So the workplace is justified as a kind of crèche-cum-skill centre, exactly as richer parents use school.

School is not a suitable place to send their children, as far as parents of some of the poorer children are concerned. Migrant workers in particular lose faith in schools, finding no point of contact between the culture on offer at school and their own culture – even the language may be different and the attitudes to migrants insulting. Why should they waste their children's energy forcing them to attend a school which they do not understand and which does not understand them? Much better the children should go to work and earn a little extra money for the family.

Schools exist, usually, to reinforce and pass on

Where schools are unwelcoming to migrant children, work seems a more useful place to go.

Work done within the family can be as harmful as exploitation by an employer.

the culture of the dominant group in society. Poor children do not slide easily into such schools – and migrant children, especially, do not. The school is faced with a choice: it can recognize that all children are a part of the community, and therefore alter its response to make every child feel welcome and able to trust that school exists for the child's benefit; or the teachers and the more privileged pupils can close ranks and make the poorer children feel it is up to them to adjust to fit in. The Italian schools inspectorate admits: 'We still have schooling which systematically discriminates against those children who are poorest and most in need of attention. Sometimes children go to work because school convinces them and their parents that they are not fit to study.'

Children pushed out of school as rejects can be drawn even by the harsh temptations of an exploitative workplace. At least they can earn a bit of money. On all these counts, then, it can seem to children as well as to parents that going out to work is not a bad idea; an improvement on hanging around street corners or getting underfoot at home.

But parents may actively welcome having their children at home if the children make themselves useful looking after the younger ones, helping on the family plot or cleaning the house. This too is a piece of economic realism: a child's domestic work is indirectly a money-earner because it frees a parent to do other work. A child may also run errands for a neighbour and earn a handful of flour or a little sugar, under the parents' supervision. Families that are very poor cannot afford to waste energy: whether that means wasting firewood or electricity or human energy. A child is a bundle of energy: a poor family puts it rapidly to use.

Work done within the family can be as inappropriate for a child's development as work done for employers. Westerners with nineteenth-century preconceptions in mind may assume that child labour must happen in workshops or down mines or in domestic service for other people; but where a child is in effect a servant at home, or a child 'helps'

on a family farm for long hours each day, that child too is at labour. Where working stunts a child in mind, heart or body, then that child is labouring. Children themselves can prefer to go out to work for an employer rather than for the family: it gives them more independence and the possibility of a little more control over their earnings, however meagre.

Work in itself, then, is not experienced by child or parent as necessarily objectionable: what is objectionable is the exploitation that may take place there. Some Western experts on children, like educationalist John Holt, go so far as to believe that a child should have the right to work instead of going to school:

The requirement that a child go to school, for about six hours a day, 180 days a year, for about ten years, whether or not he learns anything there, whether or not he already knows it or could learn it faster or better somewhere else, is such a gross violation of civil liberties that few adults would stand for it. But a child who resists is treated as a criminal.

The International Labour Organization (ILO) states, 'Not all work is necessarily harmful to children. Some activities under regulated conditions may have positive effects for the child and society.'

Most children in the world work. In traditional societies, there was no separate establishment called school; children learned adult work-skills by following their parents and other adults around from early childhood. What's wrong with this method of learning for children now? One answer is that although this response may have been appropriate in a stable society with strong social patterns, where (say) children whose parents were farmers became farmers in their turn, it is not an appropriate way to learn the wide and flexible set of skills children need to survive in a modern, urban society. Land is becoming scarce: families are making their way in their millions to cities to find themselves new kinds of jobs. Staying at home to help the parents is no longer a guarantee that a child will learn 'faster or better' what he needs or wants to learn for his own life.

A genuine, sensitive concern for the child's development is the key issue, not whether the work the child is doing is classified as 'schoolwork' or as 'work'. Work becomes labour if it hinders a child's development: labour – whether in the family, the workplace, or indeed at school – that stunts a child's growth in mind, heart or body, is exploitative and that is what we need to prevent.

'SUPER-EXPLOITATION'

A healthy, happy child is usually bursting with energy. The question is: will adults allow children to use those energies for their self-development – or

Work becomes labour when it hinders a child's development.

will adults plug into the children's energies and steal them for their own use? To take something that belongs to someone else, without their full and free consent and without due reparation, is, after all, stealing. Because children have had so few defences against adults, they cannot easily resist this stealing of their energies: that's why the growing sense that children too have rights is so important.

This doesn't mean a child should be selfish and never lend an adult a cooperative hand. Being genuinely helpful at home or in the community, as an independent person who recognizes himself willingly as an active, responsible part of a cooperative unit, is quite different from being treated as a servant; such shared activity is usually thoroughly enjoyed by children. What most children dislike is exploitation under the guise of sharing.

It happens in the most privileged of situations, not just in poverty. Take the example of the affluent Western mother who complained to her visitor that she found her daughter impossibly idle and down-in-the-mouth. But, the mother said, she had thought of a good idea to cheer the child up and help her learn to be more cooperative: she would invite her to help make a pie for the family dinner. But as the pie was being prepared, the child became gloomier and gloomier. She dropped things, worked slower. What could one do with such an unenthusiastic, lazy child? hissed the mother, as soon as the child left the room.

But the visitor had not perceived a lazy child. She had seen a girl who had begun with guarded hope, but had been given only the boring jobs to do: peeling and coring the fruit, cleaning up the utensils, while the mother kept all the creative, rewarding tasks for herself: arranging the prepared fruit, decorating the pastry. The child knew that she was being used, both as a kitchen maid and as a means of showing off to the visitor the mother's powerfully 'charitable' nature, and the child's own pathetic dependency.

But as a child brought up to know her place in a family where adults have rights over children, but children have few rights even over themselves, she had no recognized right to protest: she was required to be grateful to the mother for trying to cheer her up rather than allowed to show her rage. A child's rage is taboo, although it is often the suppressed and distorted force of her sense of autonomy; it has to be kept well battened down – and keeping the lid pushed down was consuming all the child's energy. No wonder the girl was apathetic; having to play a power game with so many cards stacked against her couldn't be other than depressing.

Power is the issue. Child labour writer Alain Morice says, 'The problem is not one of age but of exploitation.' And other child labour experts too, like Benjamin White and Victoria Goddard, begin not by accepting 'any assumed iniquity' in child labour itself but by objecting to the fact that 'children are more subordinated than adults in work relations and therefore subject to exaggerated forms of control and exploitation'.

Adults who are poor and disempowered are exploited; and because children have even less power, the children of such adults are 'super-exploited'. Apprenticeships, say child labour experts, are one way 'super-exploitation' is pursued under wraps. They may be little more than opportunities for the employer to use virtually unpaid labour. Repeating one mechanical task month after month, as Letizia did, sitting on the glueing bench in a shoe-makers' shop, does not turn a child into a craftsman or woman. But getting a foot in the workplace door through an apprenticeship can seem to children and parents like a good idea, especially where unemployment levels are very high for children when they do legally enter the job market at around fifteen. According to development writer Dexter Tiranti:

In the lines of people waiting for jobs it is young hands that are usually left idle, in rich and poor countries alike. In Syria, for example, 15–24-year-olds account for 70 per cent of the unemployed. In India they make up 67 per cent and in Ghana 60 per cent.

It is important to notice, however, that legal-age unemployment tends to be highest precisely where the use of illegal under-age labour is high – for the children have been given the jobs that their older brothers and sisters or their parents might have had, since children come cheaper and more docile. It's a vicious circle. Where the older members of a family can't get enough work, the children must be sent to earn the family bread: but if children fill up the job spaces, older people won't be employed. As Alan Whittaker of the Anti-Slavery Society says:

The sad paradox at the heart of child labour is that it perpetuates poverty because it is a cheaper alternative to already cheap adult labour. A child's wage, to an individual family, often means the difference between eating and not eating. But it is no solution in the long term. A child at work means an adult out of work and that means a smaller income. Child labour prevents the growth of organised trade unionism and maintains a Victorian-type boss's capitalism. It stunts dignity and perpetuates powerlessness.

Drying tobacco: a child at work means an adult out of work.

The ILO agrees: 'Policies aimed at promoting adult employment, raising incomes and improving living standards must be the basis for long-term action to abolish child labour.' And although many parents are relieved to have a source of supplementary energy available in their children, others realize that both generations are, in fact, caught in a trap that keeps them poor forever. But how are they to spring the trap, when they are so powerless?

THE CYCLE OF DEPRIVATION

These are the words of a father working in the appalling conditions at the glass-making furnaces at Firozabad, India:

My life is virtually over at 36. Do you think I want my son to suffer like this? If I can somehow see him through school, I'll try and keep him out of this industry. I don't want my son to die at the age of 40 years which is bound to happen to someone working 12 to 14 hours in this intense heat. But I know that I cannot work beyond another month; then how will I pay for his school clothes? If he does not have proper clothes, the teacher will not let him enter the classroom. Sooner or later, circumstances will force me to put him to work.

In some areas of Brazil nearly a third of the domestic workers are children. Some of them have been farmed out to middle-class households as servants from the age of three or four, to pay off their parents' debts. In other words, these children and their energy (24 hours a day) have been mortgaged to richer families. In India, according to the Anti-Slavery Society, a staggering five million people are bonded labourers. The chances of them ever paying off the family bond are remote: once a bonded slave, you are a slave for life – and so will your children be for theirs.

This cycle of deprivation and exploitation has to be broken, not only by governments looking after children better (by enforcing child labour laws and by making school genuinely a place where

opportunities are expanded) but by looking after workers in the family better (whether adults or children). Until then, unemployed or poorly paid parents will be blackmailed into sending their children to work, whether they or their children want to work or not. Commentators in the past have sometimes limited their perceptions of child labour to being a 'family problem' – a family that is poor has no alternative but to send their children to work. That's true up to a point: the family may indeed see no other alternative. But that doesn't mean the world at large has no alternative: it could, if it had the will, make great changes in the family's prospects.

It is not the poor family's need but the world's greed that stands as the root of the problem. An

A Moroccan girl earns a pittance for making a rug that will sell in the West for thousands of dollars.

11-year-old Moroccan girl, for instance, earns 15 cents an hour making the rug that retails in New York for several thousand dollars. Who has pocketed the difference? Not the child's family; they have seen only a pittance. Who has profited by thousands of dollars, by exploiting a poor family and 'super-exploiting' a child? Looking at the unfortunate child and her family distracts attention from the chain of exploitation that leads away from the family – and can lead right across the world.

If the child were given the profit from just one carpet that she has woven, neither she nor her family would any longer live in penury. She could afford to go to school or find some other job – she would no longer be locked into a cycle of misery and low pay from which neither she nor her own children are likely ever to be able to emerge, however hard they work. So the problem of this family's poverty is not intractable: it could be solved, through unexploitative practices at the workplace.

And if all the children who had ever knotted a carpet, or had glued a hundred pairs of shoes, or otherwise worked for a pittance that created a huge profit for someone else, had been given a fair part of the profit actually made by their labours, how many of these children and their families would now be on their way out of poverty? But these children were not given a fair share of the profits – nor will they ever be given it, until enough moral and legal pressure is put on the business community to compel them to treat their workers (of whatever age) with justice. Until then, the employers will maintain the rationalization that 'families must use their children as labourers' to survive – and the pretence that the business community is doing the families a favour by employing the children.

A bonded slave boy in India making carpets may be paid around $7 for his labour when his master is paid $225 – a 30-fold jump. That carpet may then be sold in London for up to $9,000 – this time a 40-fold jump. Even allowing for their costs, the middle-men standing between the child labourer and the customer will have scooped up a handsome profit.

And the boy will remain bonded to slavery – a bond that will almost certainly pass on to his children, and then to theirs, unless action is taken by the world community to break the chain of slave labour.

In Britain, questions were asked in 1984 about British retailers' share of responsibility for child labour in Thailand after a television programme showed Thai children forced to work 15 hours a day for as little as 40 cents, to produce clothes that were sold for a hefty profit in British high street stores. Alec Smith, General Secretary of the National Union of Tailors and Garment Workers, saw the programme and responded with passion:

What sort of a world are we living in? It is grim indeed when the only choice available to a nation's children is between prostitution and slavery. . . . The British retailer who buys from these sweating dens is as guilty as those who directly enslave these children. All their talk about getting the best deal for the consumer has been exposed as a sham. In reality, both producers and consumers are being robbed. . . .

This film must serve as a warning to all of us just what happens when the labour market is unregulated. . . . Hopefully, it will also bring home to the consumer the massive markup that takes place at the retail end of the clothing trade . . . It's time we all woke up!

The chief argument in reply to Alec Smith was that poor countries must let themselves and their children go on being exploited because they have no other choice. They can't afford to lose their foreign business – and the main bait they can offer to retailers from the rich world is their cut-price labour force. So to keep the rich business community sweet, children 'must' to on working.

But must they? Only if the business community is willing to build on the backs of prematurely ageing children, worn out by slave labour. 'In effect,' says Ed Harriman in *The New Statesman*, 'buying in Bangkok enables British firms to circumvent over 150 years of British social legislation.' It seems that the 'free' market is very expensive in children's lives.

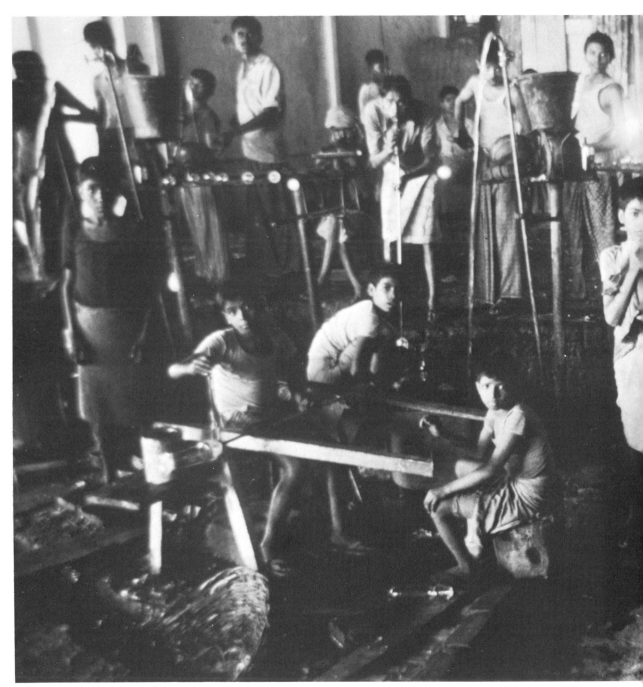

The Firozabad glassworks.

THE WORST JOBS IN THE WORLD

At least 100 million children are at labour every day, says the ILO. But Defence for Children International (DCI) claims that some estimates put the figure much higher – at 150 million in Asia alone. These estimates do not include children in the West who work at odd-jobs like baby-sitting or car-washing for extra pocket money. It includes only children who work so hard or under such poor conditions that their mental or physical health suffers.

The poignant story told by the father at the Firozabad glassworks, for example, is far from rare. Child labour specialist Dr Neera Burra gives us a taste of the conditions that parents and children suffer at these glassworks:

Most visitors to Firozabad are taken on a conducted tour of so-called model factories . . . [where] the buildings are relatively spacious; after the factory owners have told the visitor their human interest stories of poverty and child labour, one can actually leave the premises believing that the factory owners are in fact doing the poor a good turn by employing their children. If, however, one manages to visit factories other than the ones highly recommended, the conditions are truly horrifying. . . .

The whole factory floor was strewn with broken glass and naked electric wires were to be seen everywhere. The noise was deafening and there was hardly any space to move without bumping into somebody. At least 30–40 per cent of the labour force [seemed to be] children of the ages of 8–13 years. . . .

While I was watching . . . several children ran past me in a passage about 3 feet wide carrying molten glass. One worker bumped into another and part of the molten glass fell one inch away from my foot. There was no place to move because behind me were loose wires, and across this narrow passage other children were sitting on the ground with their backs to the passage in front of small furnaces, reheating the molten glass. If the molten glass (the temperature of which was nearly 1,200 °C) had not fallen near my foot, it would have fallen on a child's back.

Under these working conditions it is not surprising that industrial accidents are frequent, though government officials and factory-owners deny it.

One of the children Dr Burra met was Sriram, aged nine. He couldn't open his left eye because a piece of hot glass had flown into it. He was 'being looked after by his co-workers as his parents had left him there'. Another boy, Vijay, aged 16, had recently burned his scalp. He could not go to work for a month, and didn't get wages for that period. He borrowed money from co-workers to pay for his medical treatment.

The owners of the glass factories have no intention of letting child workers go. As one owner put it: 'The glass industry cannot function without children. They can run much faster than adults and production goes up.' Without child labour, their production would fall by 25 per cent. That's rather like saying there have to be child chimney sweeps because they are thinner than adults. What is more important, maintaining the chimney or the child? Other methods of heating houses have been found; other methods of producing glass, too, must be organized.

India is thought to have the highest population of child labourers in the world, with as many working children as there are people in the United Kingdom. But all over the world children work in horrifying conditions for people preoccupied with the bottom line and oblivious to the rights of the children. In Mexico City, according to DCI, children work sorting rubbish in a dump known as the 'Basurero de Santa Fe', which is permanently smouldering; every single child was found to suffer from skin disease, intestinal disorders and parasites. Many of these children, say DCI, are killed when they fall into fire-holes that open up in the burning mountain of trash.

In Peru, adolescents are reported to be lured from poverty-stricken Andean villages to work in the sluices of Amazonian gold fields. According to *All Work and No Play*, conditions are so bad that few live to return home. In Brazil, children work on sugar-cane plantations from the age of seven. So many children are employed that they form a sixth of the workforce. They are fed little, receiving a third of the calories they need: their poor diet significantly lowers both their mental and physical development. In Sri Lanka, child labour starts even younger. From the age of five, children are employed potting seedlings – for as little as one cent a day.

SO FAR AWAY FROM HOME

In Thailand, where as many as five million children are estimated to be exploited as child labourers, 'fisherwomen' don't catch fish: they catch children. Alan Whittaker of the Anti-Slavery Society explains:

Fisherwomen work with 'employment' agencies around Bangkok's main railway station. They are busiest during January, February and March – the dry season in Thailand, when trainloads of children aged eight or even younger arrive in the middle of the night from the provinces, sometimes alone, sometimes accompanied by other fisherwomen who seek their goods at source.

Women make the best catchers, for whom should a tired, bewildered child trust but a gently smiling matron? And these women have turned Bangkok into the world's open market in the buying and selling of children – perhaps 500 a week during the season.

The price of these young slaves usually hovers between $100 and $150, though it may be as little as $75. Receipts are issued and the living property is passed over from fisherwoman to buyer – theoretically for a year.

But no one asks for the children back and no one checks on their welfare. The child is bought for life . . . or until no longer required. When fisherwomen buy the children 'at source', they give parents in poor villages about $18 – a huge sum, says Whittaker, compared with their annual income – in exchange for finding employment for the child.

Occasionally the children manage to send pitiful messages to their parents in the north about their working and living conditions. Some are beaten by their employers, or raped. But the $18 is spent and there is no way the parents can afford to buy back the child. The children who manage to escape their employers either end up fending for themselves on

A Thai 'fisherwoman' snatches a child at Bangkok's railway station: a childhood lost to the factory or the brothel lies in store.

the streets of Bangkok as prostitutes – or collapse on the long, lonely journey home.

The Anti-Slavery Society defines child work as child labour when children are employed under conditions that are harmful to their maturing processes. The Director-General of the ILO adds another right: children must not be denied 'the right to play, to learn'. Girls, especially, are often denied time to learn or enjoy themselves, since domestic duties wipe out any free time they might have. And DCI adds that child work also becomes child labour when children are denied their fundamental right to liberty and the right to be united with their family. If this right were enforced, fisherwomen would no longer be allowed to buy children even if they sold them to well-meaning employers.

But sometimes, as we have seen in chapter 1, children are also exploited at home, so that they prefer to take their chances on the streets. The real issue, then, is not whether children use their energies at home, at school, or at work, but whether their energies are employed in any of these places in a way that is beneficial to them – or only for the benefit of someone else.

Mill girls in nineteenth-century England: child labourers, then as now, were exploited without reward for the crucial contribution they made to industrial success.

In 1833, William Cobbett made a speech in Parliament which showed how Britain was prospering at the expense of its children:

We have, Sir, this night made one of the greatest discoveries ever made by a House of Commons ... Hitherto, we have been told that our navy was the glory of the country, and that our maritime commerce and extensive manufactures were the mainstay of the realm. We have also been told that the land has its share in our greatness, and should justly be considered as the pride and glory of England. The Bank, also, has put in its claim to share in this praise, and has stated that public credit is due to it; but now, a most startling discovery has been made, namely, that all our greatness and prosperity, that our superiority over other nations, is owing to 300,000 little girls in Lancashire. We have made the notable discovery that, if these little girls work two hours less in a day than they do now, it would occasion the ruin of the country; that it would enable other nations to compete with us; and thus make an end to our boasted wealth, and bring us to beggary!

Behind the irony lies the simple fact that child labour being so undervalued brings profits to others at the children's expense. Perhaps what we need to stress, when we argue against child labour practices, is not only the exploitation of the children's vulnerability but the exploitation of the children's power – power that is used to benefit adults who already have money and status, instead of being used to benefit the child. Perhaps a better way to put a stop to child labour would be, not to bar it, but to insist on children being paid at the same, or even at a *higher*, rate than adults. Then the argument of those who say they employ small children as a 'favour' to their families may suddenly melt away.

7

THE PROTECTION RACKET

The children make the prostitutes' difficult lives impossible. At the same time, they make their lives worth living.

Ellen Aanesen

The period between a child's first and second birthday is one of the best times to be a parent. The broken nights are over – no more groggy 2 a.m. feeds – and the parent watches his child proudly as every day brings a new achievement. Standing up unaided gives way to the excitement of tottering steps, and that to exuberant bursts of running. The child's private language, which the parent has so far translated for puzzled relatives, turns into recognizable words and phrases. It is an age of congratulation and widening horizons – and the rewards of parenting start to outweigh the exhaustion.

But Princess's mother, Gina, rarely receives these rewards. Princess doesn't run around much. At 15 months, she is spindly and delicate, and holds her mother's hand anxiously as she walks. Unlike her mother, who has glossy black hair like most Filipino girls, Princess's hair is fine and brown like that of her father, a US marine whom she has never seen.

Princess looks at Gina, and doesn't smile. She has few expressions -- but then, she has not spent her life among affectionate adults who rewarded each new look. She was unwanted before she was born, has had no contact with her father or her grand-

parents and, although her mother loves her, Princess senses that she is also her mother's greatest burden. Being the child of a young prostitute has already taken a grievous toll.

But Princess's luck has begun to change. The stroke of luck may not seem like much: a night-time crèche has opened locally for the children of prostitutes. That's all – but it has signalled the beginning of a profound change in Princess's life, one that might even prevent her from having to follow her mother into prostitution.

Why should such a small change make such a big difference? To find out, we need to go back to a village in the Central Philippines, some 20 years ago.

BUT THAT WAS IN ANOTHER COUNTRY ...

Princess's mother, Gina, was born in the Visayas, a poverty-stricken area of the Philippines which is frequently devastated by typhoon and flood. Natural disasters were compounded by the Marcos government's cynical indifference to the condition of its

Gina, Princess's mother, was robbed of a healthy start in life, growing up in a rural area undeveloped by the government.

poorer people. While the government was pouring half a billion borrowed dollars into building 14 luxury hotels in the cities, it spent just 13 million dollars on housing its population.

Where Gina grew up, children rarely had enough to eat: they suffered from diseases like beri-beri which we usually associate with African famine. Infant death rates in the Visayas were high, and rising. There were no doctors or nurses to treat the village children – even the towns were lucky to have a nurse. The basic rights of children were sorely neglected. Girls like Gina knew they had no future in the provinces: they had little education, less health care and no prospect of a job.

Many girls left the region, alone, for Manila. Some found poorly paid jobs as maids or vendors; others discovered that a surer means of staying alive was to prostitute themselves. And in this they found the government and local business eager to help them. Although President Marcos publicly claimed there was no prostitution in the Philippines, his administration took steps to encourage it.

Filipinas for Sale, a booklet prepared by a women's organization in the Philippines, describes how the government set up centres where a third of a million 'hospitality girls', as they were euphemistically re-named, were 'legalized under the Philippines Labour Code as "professionals" in line with the "adoption of the tourism-oriented program"'. And by presidential decree, the Bureau of Women and Minors was re-organized: its new assignment included giving seminars to the girls on 'personality development and good grooming'.

Why was the government taking all this trouble? They weren't looking after the prostitutes for their own sakes, but for the sake of the prostitution industry: the girls were a cog turning a bigger wheel. The plan was to turn tourism into a money-spinner for the Philippines' economy, and the sexuality of young Filipinas was the bait used to lure foreign tourists into the country.

Usefully for the tour operators, the stereotyped image of Asian womanhood had a powerful hold on the Western male psyche. And the tour operators were eager to take advantage of the fantasies of men who imagined how deliciously restful it would be, after doing battle with big-boned, aggressive white women, to fall into the arms of a small, sweet, tender brown girl who knew her place.

She would have been brought up to take care of a man, to serve him rather than to make egalitarian demands of him. Personal service would go beyond domestic help: the stereotype also promised new sexual excitements. She would be a creature of exotic, liquid beauty – an idea much capitalized on in airline advertisements, which focus on the melting brown eyes and glossy lips of young air hostesses. Advertisements featuring a Western hostess may focus on her by name ('I'm Sandy – fly me'). She is a person, at least to this limited extent. But brown-skinned hostesses are shown as anonymous representatives of their birthplace ('Singapore girl'). Their charms are detached from them as persons and re-attached to their countries: the romantic invitation of the destination and of the girl's desirability are firmly intertwined.

And because the stereotypic girl on offer is presented as a de-personalized object of desire, men

For many Filipinas, working the bars as prostitutes is the only way to stay alive.

are encouraged to believe that they can try out sexual experiments on her that they wouldn't dare risk at home with a real-life, everyday wife. So not only is the Third World woman seen as a more docile kind of woman than a Western one, she is de-humanized almost out of womanhood altogether into a commodity, like a blow-up doll. One feature of a good commodity is that it can be mass-produced: tour operators used a poster featuring a desirable-looking woman (Miss Universe Margie Moran) above the caption, 'There's More Where She Comes From'.

The Bureau of Women and Minors did recognize – in a manner of speaking – that the girls' poverty was a causal factor in prostitution, and also that a moral issue was involved. To help the girls earn legal money, the Bureau handed out rosary-beading jobs before the Pope's visit in 1981. Each rosary took a girl two hours to bead and earned her half a peso from the Bureau – who re-sold it for fifty pesos. The moral issue was also tackled head on: the girls were lectured on moral values to strengthen their moral fibre, and on proper decorum 'so that the men will learn to respect you'.

The official 'protectors', clearly, were the girls' chief exploiters.

The Marcos government used the sexuality of Filipino boys and girls to lure tourists to the country.

RIGHTS AND OBLIGATIONS

The police willingly joined in the 'protection racket'. A curfew was imposed on children unaccompanied by parents at night, supposedly to stop child prostitution. But if a child prostitute was caught, her pimp would pay off the police at once and she would be back on the beat straightaway. Children who could not pay 'would be carted off to police outposts where they were usually raped or abused while in detention', says *Filipinas for Sale*. It is the regular complaint of children who survive on the street in many countries: the police are not there to protect them, but take advantage of their vulnerability to use them for sex.

In principle, adults have power over children (whether we mean toddlers or teenagers) not because adults are intrinsically more valuable than children but because we believe adults need extra powers in order to look after children properly. If an adult

says 'no' to a small child crawling up to touch a fire, we respect his right to restrict the child because it springs from a mature sense of responsibility; that doesn't apply if an adult says 'no' to a child merely in order to assert his superiority. That's just bullying.

So adults are granted power over children as an adjunct of their *obligation* towards children: it is not something justified outside this context. And children, correspondingly, have the *right* to expect this adult obligation towards them to be fulfilled. As Paul Sieghart writes in *The Lawful Rights of Mankind*:

Rights and duties are symmetrical. It is a popular fallacy to believe that this symmetry applies within the same individual: that if I have a right, *I* must also have a correlative duty. This is not so: if I have a right, *someone else* must have a correlative duty; if I have a duty, *someone else* must have a corresponding right.

The child does not need to 'deserve' or 'qualify for' this obligation to be looked after: being a child is entitlement enough. Children have rights 'by right' and not through desert – and this principle of an intrinsic adult obligation and a corresponding child entitlement is reinforced by the Convention on the Rights of the Child.

But the Marcos government, in power over thousands of Filipino children like Gina, clearly failed in their obligation to them. It did not ensure that the children in their care had their basic needs honoured, needs for food, for health care, for education, or even to be able to live with their families. It failed them to the point where the children had to find their own ragged routes to survival in faraway cities. And worse: the government's failure to meet its obligations – betrayal by omission – was followed by a betrayal by commission. It actively took advantage of the children's lack of minimal rights to exploit their vulnerability, by using them as tourist bait. In this way, the government betrayed the children twice over.

Tourists came, duly lured, not only from the United States and Europe but from the nearest

Children picked up by the police for being in the red light district at night.

wealthy country – Japan. One tour operator explained that he would charter a bus, collect about $100 per Japanese tourist and drive over to an exclusive club where there would be at least 200 numbered girls or young women. The tourists would choose their partners for the night by writing down their numbers. They paid an average of $60 a night, of which only $10–20 trickled down to the girl. The rest was divided between the club owner, the tour operator, the Filipino guide and the Japanese guide.

Homosexual tourists, too, made a bee-line for the Philippines, alerted by child sex guides. The best known was the Spartacus Gay Guide, a 600-page volume that gave names and addresses of establishments in 150 countries where boys could be found

without risk. Sri Lanka was another favourite hunting ground for white pedophiles, where the boys' specialities were listed and customers advised to book the most popular children well in advance.

The best known place in the Philippines for pedophiles was Pagsanjan. Most people in this small town of 20,000 knew what was going on and looked the other way. The *Christian Science Monitor* interviewed Hannie Rogers, a Dutch-Indonesian woman who had recently moved to Pagsanjan. She couldn't believe what she was seeing. 'It made me angry because I knew these men could not get away with anything like this back where they came from', she said. 'I saw how these children here were exploited by people from First World countries.'

But it wasn't just the foreigners who were exploiting the children of the Philippines, whether boys or girls. The Filipino government, which had a clear duty to protect its youth, was also prostituting it for financial gain. The prostitutes, and sometimes the customers, were blamed while the businessmen and the politicians who oiled the wheels of the prostitution industry stayed in the background, making their profits. Occasionally a brothel-keeper would be fined a derisory sum.

The commercial ethic, when separated from human ethics, subverts every quality of goodness into a product with a price-tag. The freshness and vulnerability of children, qualities that normally touch adult hearts and rouse protectiveness, become re-framed as a chance for greater profits when seen through the cold eye of commercialism: the more innocent, the more profitable. Virgins fetch their pimps the biggest price.

When Corazon Aquino overthrew the Marcos regime, she wanted the government to stop playing pimp to its children. The Aquino administration has dropped the Marcos hypocrisy of pretending that prostitution doesn't exist in the Philippines while encouraging 'hospitality girls'. Instead the new government openly admits that there are 15,000 street children in Manila, of whom they reckon some 30 per cent engage in prostitution.

In June 1986, the Philippines government declared a 'Year of the Exploited Child', to open up the issue of child prostitution to discussion and research. They recognize that the pervasive climate of acceptance has to be dissolved and replaced by a new public ethos, in which children have their rights to protection from sexual exploitation unambiguously upheld. The change hasn't happened yet. For most of the street children today, the climate in Manila remains the old commercial one: if you have something to sell, you sell it; if all you have to sell is your body, you sell that – and good luck to you.

Manila also provides a grapevine for rumours of places where more money is to be had – like Olongapo, a new town that has mushroomed around the US naval base at Subic Bay. Thousands of Americans, with beautiful dollars burning holes in their pockets, are said to be stationed permanently at the base – with thousands more coming and going on US naval ships and planes. Like bees to honey, hundreds of hungry young men and women have been collecting their belongings and heading hopefully for Olongapo, some from Manila, and some directly from the countryside, Gina among them.

SEX IN SUBIC BAY

Sleek grey ships rest in the waters of Subic Bay. They belong to the US 7th fleet, which regularly pulls into the naval base for the ships to be repaired and for the servicemen to enjoy 'R&R' – rest and

When the ship comes in: 7,000 US soldiers hit the bars of Olongapo.

recreation. Overhead, the skies shiver with the sound of US fighter planes. These airmen, too, go in search of R&R.

About 7,000 men seek out R&R in the city every day, and the chief leisure requirement of these men is women. The navy is solicitous of the needs of the weary men, though they are not about to recreate family life. And the local government is eager to be hospitable. Between them, the naval and the local authorities make sure the servicemen have a good time.

Some 500 bars, hotels and massage parlours line the streets leaving the main gate of Subic base. And to reduce the possibility of the men who use these facilities catching venereal disease, the city government and the US Navy run the Social Hygiene Clinic at Olongapo as a joint project: the salaries of the staff are paid by the city while the Navy provides free medicines, laboratory work and technical advice. The Clinic's job is to give the local women and girls medical checks. If they pass the medical, they are given registration cards to prove they are free of disease. More than 5,000 women in the city of Olongapo are on the register. A further 10,000 unregistered prostitutes live in Olongapo or in other towns nearby.

When Gina arrived in Olongapo, she found that there were virtually no jobs to be had that didn't involve working in one of these 500 alcohol-and-sex parlours. From there it was a short step to prostitution. The bar owners offered Gina little or no salary for any other work: dancers earned only 20 pesos ($1) per night of dancing. Waitresses and entertainers were paid no salary at all. And some of the 'entertainments' were no better than prostitution. When the ships were in, women were covered in oil and expected to wrestle or box each other in front of the servicemen, or forced to do vaginal tricks: in the commonest, the men placed peso coins on top of a beer bottle for a woman to suck into her vagina. Other tricks involved vaginal egg-breaking or cigarette-smoking. To blot out their shame, many of these women took drugs.

Prostitution could hardly seem worse. But even prostitution, Gina found out, had its extra humiliations. Gina didn't earn money directly from customers: as a bar girl she was an employee of the bar owner. He received the money (known as a 'bar fine') from the customer and later Gina would be given her share, perhaps half or a third of the bar fine. And the smallest infraction of the barman's rules lost her even that: being five minutes late for a meeting, taking a day off without permission (women work seven days a week), or *even failing to join a pro-base rally* was enough. Gina found that it was not only her body that had been bought: even her thoughts were not allowed to be her own.

She was certainly not allowed to refuse a man. Even if she accepted him but the serviceman was unsatisfied with her performance, he could demand his money back. Not only did Gina then lose her commission, she had to pay the rest of the bar fine herself, out of other money she had earned. So she could not even protect herself by switching off and offering her body passively – she had to turn in an enthusiastic performance, or be penalized for showing her distaste.

The bar fine system guarantees the bar owner his money and the serviceman his satisfaction – and in return guarantees the prostitute nothing. She must deliver the goods without fail: be available every day, on time, always to the required standards. If she fails in any of these ways, even if the reasons are beyond her control, the responsibility is placed at her door and the consequences are borne by her. No reciprocal responsibility is taken by the employer or the customer for Gina. If she catches a disease or becomes pregnant, frequent occupational hazards, or even grows old and looks past her sexual prime, she is abandoned. And even if her daughter Princess is sick – as she often is, since she is fed on bottled milk – and cries for her mother to stay with her that night, just for once, Gina cannot stay without being fined or fired.

In all these ways, then, Gina's job turned out to be a kind of slavery, for all the obligations went

The night shift girls have no rights: they are trapped into a kind of slavery.

only in one direction. Gina had always to fulfil her obligations – but neither the employer nor the customer felt any obligation towards her. So the physical and emotional degradation of being used sexually by strangers was only part of the misery of her existence: what was as bad was that Gina had literally been 'de-graded' from human being to slave, or even to object. Her body was like a room rented out or a machine for hire. Her intrinsic rights, her reality as a human being, were of no interest.

If any notice was taken of her, it was to despise her. In the words of Brenda Stolzfus, who initiated the night-care shelter for babies like Princess:

'Church, society, and the customers themselves look down on the women, seeing them as sinners.' In an extraordinary act of scapegoating, the young women are seen as sinners by the very men who are 'sinning' with them, and enjoying every minute of it.

SCAPEGOATS FOR SOCIETY

Prostitutes are scapegoats for the sexual hypocrisy of society. Virtually the whole of Olongapo is involved in the bar business, despite the 'hospitality women' taking the rap. The affluent pillars of the citizenry, members of the Lions' Club or the Rotary Club, are owners of bars and have their own Bar Owners' Association. Even the seamstresses, respectably sewing clothes for the servicemen all day in the tailoring shops, usually supplement their tiny incomes at night by selling their bodies.

You can see scapegoating in action in yet another condition placed on Gina by her employers: she must carry her Social Hygiene Clinic's registration card, like a label on a supermarket pack that shows fitness for human consumption. Every other week, Gina has to return to the Clinic for VD smears; twice a year she must have a chest X-ray. All these costs she has to pay herself. If a man demands to see her health card, she must be able to show it to him. She is not allowed to refuse to show it, and she can't ask him for a card as proof of his health. Men are not subjected to these tests and carry no cards.

The assumption in Olongapo, then, is that it is women who spread disease and men who are their vulnerable victims – despite the fact that the men do not restrict themselves to registered women; they also avail themselves of the 10,000 unregistered street prostitutes within easy reach of the base. They do not even restrict their sexual activities to the Philippines – it is the customers who have introduced AIDS to the women of Olongapo from abroad.

The myth that women, not men, are the unclean spreaders of disease is not peculiar to Olongapo, or to the Philippines – or even to the Third World. Everywhere the blame is placed on women. Anthropologist Judith Ennew gives the example of West Germany's municipally organized 'eros centres'; the same mythology applies and it is the women prostitutes who are tested for disease, not their customers.

Filipina prostitutes who catch venereal diseases from their male customers have nowhere to go. Since there is no one to look after them but themselves, they have no safety net beyond their own daily efforts to survive. A sick woman, or a woman who can no longer bear to prostitute herself, is a woman with no income. Adora, one of Gina's friends, is a seamstress who became pregnant twice through prostitution. She can't face the thought of offering herself to a customer again – but now she has three mouths to feed on her earnings as a seamstress. It was an income that didn't support her well enough on her own – that was why she turned to selling sex – and by no means can it support three. Often, Adora cannot afford to feed her children, or to rent them a room. Then Gina takes them in: two young mothers and three children squeeze into one small room with no window and no electricity.

Gina knows that at present she stands on the lowest rung of the job-ladder. But if she catches a venereal disease, she will slip off even that rung and then she – and Princess – must starve. Servicemen who catch VD are cared for at the base.

What about personal support systems? When the state or the employer doesn't help, young people usually turn to their parents or partners for assistance. These personal support systems too are harder for a prostitute to rely on, because of the taint of their 'sinfulness'. Few men are willing to marry a known prostitute, and Gina lies to her mother about her job. She tells her that she was married to an American who fathered Princess but unfortunately died soon after. She would like Princess to visit her grandparents, but is nervous that her job will be found out and that she and Princess will be rejected. They have already been rejected too many times to bear more rejection.

As soon as Gina confessed her pregnancy, she was fired. And when Gina's steady boyfriend realized that she was pregnant by an American, he rejected her too. While her job carries such a moral stigma against her – rather than against her customers, against her employers or against a social system that forces her into such work – Gina cannot justify herself to those who despise her. She cannot even justify herself convincingly to herself.

Says Brenda Stoltzfus:

Hospitality women bear the double burden of societal degradation of their work and promotion of the prostitution industry for its income generation. They deeply internalize the degradation and de-humanization. . . . Some become depressed to the point of attempting suicide. Others finally conclude that they are being played with and in order to survive must play the game back. Playing the game may mean presenting a 'hardened' outer shell, and trying to bury the pain deep inside, or it may mean getting everything they can by stealing money when the customer is asleep.

The dream of the prostitutes is to marry an American. That would legitimize their lives once more. 'They could be real people again,' as Stoltzfus puts it. 'It is the dream that sweetens the reality for the women of Olongapo who cling around the base.' They see life in the United States as providing opportunities for their children, so that they will not have to follow in their mothers' sad footsteps.

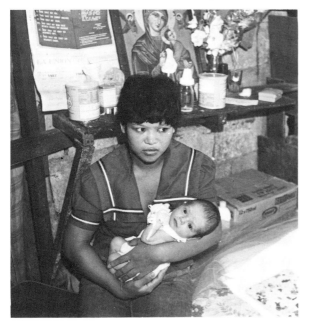

Young prostitute with child, fathered by a US marine.

PROSTITUTES AS MOTHERS

It was when Gina first became pregnant that her troubles multiplied too fast for her to handle. She opted to risk a back-street abortion, despite the heavy anti-abortion pressure in a Catholic country. It was a horrendous experience. When she became pregnant again, this time with Princess, the nightmarish memories stopped her considering abortion again. But how was she to manage with a baby? She couldn't work when she was very pregnant – in any case, the bar owner simply sacked her when her pregnancy became known – and in her vulnerable state she needed shelter.

Alone and penniless, Gina found herself in the sort of situation we usually associate with Dickensian melodrama, though it is no fiction for thousands of young women. Gina threw herself on the mercy of her landlord and landlady, who agreed to let her fall behind with her rent – on condition that Gina swapped the baby for her debt.

Seeing no other way out, Gina agreed – and then made a telling amendment to the deal: if the baby were a girl, she would exchange her for her debt. If it were a boy, Gina wanted to keep him. There is no clearer evidence than this of the effect of living in a social system where everyone deeply accepts the myth of male superiority; where everyone submits to the belief that women should give their power away to men – even the very women whose lives have been wrecked by the power imbalance.

At the hospital, Gina successfully negotiated the birth, despite her poverty and isolation. 'Giving birth can be a traumatic experience for hospitality women,' says Stoltzfus, 'due to lack of funds for the hospital care. If they have no money they are often treated badly at the local general hospital.'

None the less, the process of childbirth brought about a profound change in Gina, as it does in many women. For the first time in her life, Gina had irrefutable, tangible evidence of her value: she had grown in her body and delivered into life *a baby*. However much she might be despised and degraded

Who will look after a bar girl's baby when she is earning money to keep them both alive?

the baby was a girl, she would not part with her. Now, of course, she had a child as well as a debt – two mouths to feed and no way to earn money without leaving the child with a baby-sitter, who would also demand to be paid. And leaving Princess with a sitter meant feeding her bottled milk, which cost an enormous amount and gave the baby diarrhoea – which meant that the baby-sitter didn't want to look after her. Gina was angry and frustrated: she couldn't bear the thought of her baby being constantly 'abandoned', as she put it, by the sitter – a response she must have felt very deeply, having been abandoned by so many people herself – and yet she couldn't stay home to look after the child, not earning money, for then they would both starve.

The landlady kept pressing her for the money or the child. 'All your debt will be gone, because you are giving your child to me . . .' But Gina resisted. 'I said to her, that is not possible. I said, you are a mother. You have also had a difficult time – yet you would take my child, just like that! I said, you will have to wait until the time I can pay you back the money – *do you expct me to give you higher priority than my child?*'

Says Defence for Children International:

It is the very vulnerability of children that provides almost all adults with the opportunity to demonstrate their ability to succeed in a task that carries with it a universally high level of social approval. To be recognized by one's peers as a good and caring parent – whatever the cultural definition of this might be – raises the self-esteem of the poorest peasant, the most exploited worker or the member of the lowest caste.

Conversely, to be condemned as a neglectful parent . . . can carry with it a devastating social stigma. It matters not that the social pressures on the parents may be tremendous and outside of their own control. The feelings of guilt that result from an inability to care for one's child are tremendous.

by others, she had produced a new and miraculous expression of her own creativity; Princess existed, a living 'expression' of Gina's female power.

'Bearing and giving birth to a child is a marvellous act of creation – giving birth to another human being. It is something no man can do,' says psychotherapist Dr Nick Hedley. 'No wonder some men become jealous. But a woman can do it, even if she has no self-esteem and feels she has nothing else to offer. Giving birth can be a transformative experience.'

During the birth of Princess, Gina changed her mind about the deal with her landlady. Although

How could Gina give Princess away? In every way she had been disadvantaged by society and marked down as bad. At last she had the chance to demonstrate her goodness – 'I would have no conscience as a mother if I left her'; she had someone to love and care for, and someone who would, she believed, love and care for her when she was old. Life was no longer only about exploitation and isolation; there was continuity, interdependence, love – some fragment of personal meaning. And as importantly, bringing up a child, like giving birth to a child, offered Gina a purpose in life beyond mere survival. As she put it: 'I am able to see my effectiveness, I am able to raise her, send her to school.' What she earns would at least have a dignifying aim, if not a dignified source.

Ellen Aanesen, who made a film for the 'Stolen Childhood' television series about the prostitutes in Olongapo, was strongly moved by the experience. She said:

The Buklod night-care centre for the babies of prostitutes.

There are few places on earth where the conditions for real and honest love are less favourable than in Olongapo. There is hardly a place you can hear and see the word 'love' more often, from the roaring juke-boxes and on every sign. There is hardly a place where the word 'love' is more worn out, and deprived of its meaning. The prostitutes' relationship to their children seemed to be one of the few sources of real love.

But for all her good intentions, to look after Princess seemed logistically impossible. It was at this point that Gina heard about the night-care centre at Buklod for the babies of prostitutes.

SPRINGING THE TRAP

The Buklod night-care centre opened in July 1988 as a pilot project of the National Council of Churches in the Philippines, funded by Redd Barna (Norway's branch of the Save the Children Fund). The extraordinary thing about Buklod for Gina was that it was free. For once in her life, there wasn't a commercial angle – no one was trying to exploit her. All

Gina had to do was to bring Princess and her food there each evening, and collect her in the morning.

And Buklod was unjudgemental. No one at Buklod criticized her for being a prostitute, or tried to persuade her to leave the life. For the first time, Gina had the experience of entitlement: she had a place at the centre for Princess by right, as a mother with a baby in need, rather than through 'deserving' it by adherence to some impossible morality. She had the taste of being a person with recognized human rights – and Princess had her first taste of her needs and rights as a child being honoured by someone other than her mother.

Gina thinks that at last she may be able to spring the trap she is in. She can save a little money each week, now, to pay off her debts. Before Princess is old enough to ask questions about where her mother goes at night, she wants to be able to start a new life. She has seen what happens to other prostitutes whose children grow up in Olongapo. One girl followed her mother into prostitution when her mother couldn't earn enough; another one's young son ran away and, heart-breakingly, has not been seen again; another has a little girl of ten who insists she does not know what women can do for a living besides cook or nurse – though later shame-facedly admits to knowing that 'hostesses' go to hotels with men. She cannot bring herself to add that this is what her mother does.

The staff at Buklod don't want prostitution to continue in Olongapo: they see clearly how it has been institutionalized in this city, and how de-humanizing a system it is. But they are not swooping down to rescue the young prostitutes from their jobs – that, too, would be an arrogant and disem-powering act, suggesting that the prostitutes are helpless victims. On the contrary, they recognize that the prostitutes have been heroic in their struggle to survive within the very limited options they have had.

The Buklod staff's intention is to improve the environment within which the young prostitutes make their choices – for example, by raising the level of awareness among the public about the national and international system which uses and abuses these girls, and by linking up with a local college where they can further their education. The wider society can, they hope, be encouraged to recognize its obligations towards these young mothers and their children.

And they also hold the corresponding hope: that the prostitutes will use Buklod as a way of empower-ing themselves – by using it as a drop-in centre where they can break down their painful isolation and form mutual support groups. They have already taken over much of the running of the centre. Eventually they may run centres like Buklod all over the country. And then what might these women do with their lives? Whatever they choose to do, they have a better chance of enabling their own children not to be forced into following in their footsteps. They will be able to give their children a better start through their own efforts, not by hoping a rich foreigner in a sleek ship will sail them away from it all.

THE IMPORTANCE OF ENTITLEMENT

The distinction experienced by Gina at Buklod, between *having needs met by right or through deserving*, is the key to a child's freedom from exploitation. Until a child (or a young woman barely grown out of childhood) holds this key in her hand, she is trapped in the belief that she needs to *deserve* having her needs met. If she sees herself as bad or inferior in some way (as she is bound to, as a prostitute in a scapegoating society), if she feels guilty or ashamed, she will imagine that she doesn't

For Gina and the other bar girls, the Buklod centre is a first step towards gaining their rights.

really deserve to have her needs met; she has no right to a just life.

Getting her needs met, then, depends on her being acceptable to those who have power over her; she must be redeemed as 'good' through their approval. Her sense of rights dissolves and she becomes a sort of mendicant, who begs for approval and money to survive, as a gift from those above.

In a gift relationship, the person in the relationship who has the power gives gifts *at his discretion* to the one who is powerless, as long as she is vulnerable and genuflecting. Thus the power imbalance is perpetuated, and the cycle goes on. Only by a realization of her rights – often a sudden, outraged awakening to a sense of entitlement – can the victim in this system come to her senses and see that there is another way to survive than through dependence on those who appear to have the power.

We can't blame a child for prostituting herself like this: it is the pattern of society everywhere. Whole countries willingly prostitute themselves. Touting for tourists, they prostitute their national cultures in a tawdry bargain that reduces national customs and festivals to seasonal performances. As flashing camera bulbs capture temple ceremonies, meaning is forgotten and reverence becomes irrelevant – though nobody minds as long as the dollars keep rolling in.

We all prostitute ourselves to one degree or another in order to become acceptable to other people: we 'buy love' by going to family gatherings we don't want to go to, taking presents we don't want to give; we choose jobs we think will buy us approval from society or family rather than taking the risk to do the job we feel called inwardly to do; we marry people we know we shouldn't to please him (or her), or the family. Prostitution doesn't have to have anything to do with sex; any way in which we give away our best, our truest selves, in order to buy comfort and approval is a form of prostituting ourselves.

Sexual prostitution is an extreme form of this betrayal, with complications: and, in the case of child prostitutes, a far more forgivable form – for they allow the betrayal of what they could be not, as we do, in order to have a quiet life, but in order to survive.

ABUSE BY CONSENSUS

Though we may forgive the prostituted child, the abuser who steals a childs' sexuality is less easy to forgive. If a child is to believe that she (or he) is entitled – and expected – to refuse sexual exploitation, she must obviously be supported in this belief

A handful of women: a favourite T-shirt in Subic Bay.

by the consensus of the adults around her. But in reality the international community, the nation, and sometimes even her own family have supported an opposite belief: that the use of a child's sexuality for an adult's gratification is permissible. Some parents openly rely on their daughters and sons to provide the major part of the family income through selling sex. And a community is often willing to turn a blind eye to what goes on in the shadows while child sex earns the community money. All these networks have joined to steal the children's sexuality.

Prostitution performs another important function for the community, beyond earning money. It relieves the pressure of repressed sexual desires in the community. By relying on children to 'take on the dirty work', it allows the rest of the community to see itself as 'staying clean'. The community uses the prostitute (who is 'outside' the community) in order to maintain a coherent and worthy identity in its own eyes. Some parents, similarly, use their children to keep the shadow of their unacceptable sexual desires hidden within the family walls; and people who are unable or unwilling to use their own children may move on to other people's children whom they can pick up outside a family's protective walls, like Melissa or Iain whom we met in chapter 2. If even these children seem to be too much like 'their own kind' to abuse, or if they are too difficult to abuse without danger of exposure, the adults' answer seems to be to go on a sex tour abroad.

The systematic use of children to gratify adult sexual appetites goes on the world over. Sometimes the psychological sadism – inherent in any relationship where one person calculatedly uses another – spills over into physical sadism. In Brazil, for example, Renee Bridel and Jean-Paul Collomp report that 12- to 15-year-old children are taken to centres called 'maisons d'abattage' in remote parts of the country. These houses are guarded by police dogs and barbed wire; armed guards forbid access to anyone not known to the owner. Here the children are said to be drugged heavily and forced to submit to as many as 80 sexual acts with men a day, and beaten if they resist. They are later sent to other centres where they are treated less sadistically – but threatened with being sent back to the first centre if they disobey.

Children are exploited worldwide not only for use as prostitutes, but in pornography – and they are even bought and sold for sex. Defence for Children International (DCI) describes recruiters who seek out children to buy for delivery to brothels. They also describe auctions where girls are sold – for example in Karachi in 1983, a slave market was held where women and girls kidnapped from Sri Lanka and Bangladesh were sold into prostitution, most likely, DCI says, to Arab countries.

There are known routes, they claim, for the export and import of children: annually, about 8–10,000 young girls are brought from Thailand to Japan to be used in prostitution; Nepalese children are kidnapped and brought to brothels in India; and Hong Kong apparently receives girl prostitutes from the Philippines and Thailand. And under the guise of marriage bureaux, young women are procured from South-East Asia for consumption in Western Europe. In 1977, about 2,000 Thai women were brought to the Federal Republic of Germany; today, DCI believes, half of them are working as prostitutes.

How many children are sexually exploited for commercial purposes worldwide is not known. Estimates vary from hundreds of thousands of children to millions. The lack of knowledge stems partly from the difficulty of tracking down such clandestine dealings – but also from two other difficulties: one, if organizations like governments or powerful vice rings (there are constant rumours of Mafia connections) are profiting from child sex, then the motivation to make thorough, large-scale investigations is dampened; and two, countries and communities often don't want pulled out into the light of day the murky realities hidden in their shadows. They prefer to make the murk 'disappear' by denying it exists – or by making out it only exists in aberrant cases, rather than facing that it is part of their social system.

It is clear from Gina's story, however, as well as from the thousands of stories now accumulating about girls and boys around the world, that children are sexually exploited not by a handful of peculiar strangers invading a fundamentally child-protective community, but by whole communities who silently consent to the damage done to their children; often it is the people challenging the prevailing climate of acceptance who are themselves denounced.

In Olongapo in 1982, for example, two 12-year-old girls found their way to the nuns at the John XXIII Hospital for treatment. They had wounds and painful eruptions all over their bodies, and

could hardly walk. The nuns discovered ten other girls – aged eight to 12 – in a similar state. They needed treatment for syphilis, gonorrhoea, genital herpes and wounds around the neck. Father Shea Cullen, who ran a centre for child drug addicts, heard the children describe how they had been forced to work for a prostitution ring whose existence the municipal authorities had tried to cover up.

The ring-leaders offered the children to a petty officer from the naval base who used them for himself and his friends. 'For 10 dollars they submitted to sexual relations, but for 25 dollars they could be tied to chairs, beaten, slapped and subjected to mock strangulation. They were taken to the customer after having been raped or drugged or both.'

When the affair came to the attention of the press, the American petty officer was sentenced to gaol – for a matter of *months* – and the Philippine ring-leaders were not charged. But Father Cullen was threatened with expulsion for having brought the 'good name of the town' into disrepute.

IN NEED OF A MEDIA-STORM

It is important to note the role of the media here. Had it not been for press exposure, nothing at all might have happened. Children need – and are entitled by right – to have the brilliant spotlight of the world's attention focus on their sexual torture. Sexual exploitation must not be allowed to go on any longer in the shadows, under the guise of 'hospitality' bars or behind barbed wire.

The International Association of Democratic Lawyers (IADL), which has been pursuing cases of child trafficking, agrees that public awareness and the interest of the mass media are the most potent weapons against abusers: 'Those who are guilty of crime against children must be made aware that one day they will be made responsible, and that every possible kind of publicity will be procured to throw light on the serious outrages they have committed.' Judith Ennew suggests that UNICEF takes a leading role in combating the problem. And Alf Anderson, in his report on international child sexual exploitation for the Norwegian Department of Justice, demands 'a media-storm and the rage of world opinion'.

Until the world is made to look and to mind, we will indulge in the luxury of pretending that a few deranged monsters attack a few unfortunate child victims – while the sexual suffering continues of hundreds of thousands of children all over the world.

8

A UNIQUE HUMAN BEING

I must always be good and measure up to the norm, then there is no risk; I constantly feel that the demands are too great, but I cannot change that, I must always achieve more than others.

From A. Miller, The Drama of Being a Child

As soon as Martina was born, her mother Berit sensed that something must be wrong even before she saw the baby. The usual murmurs of congratulation were missing, and the softening of faces when a child is born.

Instead, the doctors took Berit straight into a separate room where she had little contact with the other patients – and soon afterwards she was allowed to take Martina to their home near Stockholm. Three times during the next three months Berit went back to the hospital nursery, still anxious that all was not well: 'I could tell from Martina's eyes that something was wrong.'

At the end of the three months the doctors were at last prepared to tell Martina's parents what the problem was. The moment of truth was brusque when it finally came. 'The doctor said that Martina was "mongoloid", and that there was no hope for her. That it was idiocy.' Berit is bruised by the brutality of the moment. 'He used that word. I remember especially well that he used a word with "idiot" in it.'

Martina was born with one chromosome too many, a condition known as Down's Syndrome. And what were Martina's parents advised to do about their 'idiot' child? The advice was stark. Berit recalls the doctor's words: 'He said to forget her. He said that we were young, with good jobs, and that we should forget about *this* as quickly as possible. He suggested we had another baby at once.' And Martina? She was to be given up permanently into residential state care.

THE FLAWLESS TOMATO

Rejected infants, in some ancient societies, were sentenced to death through exposure on the mountainside or being trampled to death under the feet of blindfolded bullocks. In the nineteenth century infanticide was replaced with a sanitized, symbolic death: 'imperfect' infants were shut away in large, residential institutions where they spent the rest of their meaningless lives, fed and clothed by the state and forgotten by their family. This new response saved the public the trouble of avoiding people with disabilities while salving its conscience with the thought that they were being properly looked after.

But in the late twentieth century, people are uneasy about putting children away in institutions. Children, even 'imperfect' children, are being recognized as more than bodies, as spirit as well as matter. Is segregation and institutionalization an act of violence to the human spirit? As the inner life of children becomes included in our understanding, we sympathize with parents like Berit who refused to treat her child as an object whose value depended on its market perfection. We recoil at the thought that Berit has been expected to treat Martina like a toaster which she bought at the hospital-shop, found to be faulty beyond repair, and for which she is therefore allowed by the doctor–shopkeeper to choose a replacement object (at no extra cost to the customer).

Martina at the age of five: her mother saw the potential for cultivating the 'inner child'.

In *Sex and Destiny*, Germaine Greer quotes an ABC television programme in 1978 where two guests debated the possibility of babies being grown in artificial wombs. One of them could hardly wait for the day:

Yes, yes. I foresee it with urgent approval. . . . I should be eager for the day when I could actually see, let's say through a glass container, a conceptus develop from fertilisation through to term. . . . Artificial gestation . . . in such a non-uterine container is the most desirable thing in the world for me to imagine.

But the other guest, a Dr Helleger, had anxieties about 'the increasing objectivisation of children . . . children as a product of artifice. I think it's already terribly difficult for an American child today to come home with a C-minus instead of an A. . . . This intolerance towards imperfection, I have some considerable misgivings about.'

And Greer herself comments:

The 'objectivisation' or reification of which Dr Helleger was speaking is already far advanced. . . . Reproduction in the highly developed world has become a kind of manufacture; doctors do not want children for themselves, they want children just as industry demands a better mousetrap, or a bigger, brighter, more regularly formed, utterly flawless (and tasteless) tomato.

Berit wasn't interested in taking home a perfect consumer product in the form of a child; she was interested in mothering a real baby, flaws and all. Anyway, by whose lights was Martina flawed? Compared to what model of correctness? Berit refused to give up her daughter and began a long fight for her to be treated as a human being rather than as a reject, focusing on her abilities rather than her disabilities. As Tom Alandh, a friend of the family who filmed Martina at five-yearly intervals, said: 'She saw Martina's possibilities rather than the problems.'

Gradually, through singing and music and games, side by side with her younger brother, Martina learned to speak. She was allowed to attend a day-care centre with normal children because she was considered to be unusually bright for a child with Down's Syndrome: but would she have become so bright if she had been institutionalized? Berit had scooped Martina up from a downward spiral of low expectation producing low performance, and placed her instead on a spiral going up.

After the day-care centre, Martina went on to a normal nursery school, once again because of her mother Berit's determination, and from there to a Montessori school and then elementary school and junior high, all the time with normal children. As long as she was allowed to work at her own speed, according to her own ability, Martina managed.

But to get people at each stage to give Martina a chance was always a struggle. Berit expressed her frustration in a poem:

> I must shout, shout out loud,
>   have the strength to keep shouting
>   that you *can* do things
>   and want to do them
>   if we believe that you can and want to,
> And we will give you a humane life.
>
> You unique little person
>   who always gives your affection
>   with no demands,
> Under whose conditions are you to exist?

TRAINING A CIRCUS HORSE

Martina herself has not been oblivious to the constant resistance around her. As a sensitive child she found painful the unresponsiveness and lack of belief that surrounded her. Now, as a young woman of 20, Martina looks back on a childhood where she often shed tears in her bedroom, where her mother would not see how sad she was. Martina was aware of how stingingly her mother felt the pain Martina experienced, worse than if it were her own.

And what about Martina's own confidence? When other people make it evident they think she is different from the desirable norm, does that make her believe she is different too? Martina reflects carefully on the question as she answers: 'I don't feel I am different *directly*. But yes, sometimes I feel sad I have my disability . . . Quite often I wonder why I have it. I'd like to be normal.'

Her honesty is painful to hear. A film of her at the age of ten finds her dancing at a class party with her arms around a classmate's neck and his arms tightly clasped around her; it shows just how well she was accepted by other children. But however successfully Martina integrates herself with other children, she is not allowed by the adults who run society to forget that she is considered abnormal – perceived as belonging outside the circle identified as properly human.

One academic went so far as to dismiss the education of Martina as being like the training of a circus horse. A circus horse can do tricks but he doesn't really understand what's going on; his cleverness isn't evidence of an inner understanding and a wish to express that understanding: his tricks only demonstrate someone else's intelligence imposed on him. Is Berit imposing on Martina by refusing to see Martina's disabilities?

Or is it the academic who is refusing to recognize Martina's abilities? One day when Martina was playing the piano, her brother shouted to her from the other room: 'Martina, you shouldn't play that so well. You must remember that you are mentally retarded!' Martina giggles at the recollection: 'That was the best thing I ever heard.'

Berit is fierce in her belief that we should be wary of imposing limits and standards, for we may not be aware whose limits we are accepting, and by what criteria those limits are decided. 'We put labels on people,' she says. 'We put them into categories like "mentally retarded". I think it is very dangerous to do that – because behind every intellectually disabled person is a human being. And all human beings are unique.' This is one of Berit's essential

Nothing gives Martina more pleasure than playing the piano.

contributions: her refusal to be blinded by stereo-types. She insists on seeing real people, and not the boxes within which prejudice places them.

Berit is well aware that Martina does have intellectual limitations. She describes her, for example, as a 'here-and-now child', for Martina has little sense of time and she doesn't worry about the future. For Berit this creates an extra responsibility – though for Martina it may be a useful mechanism: it allows her to live in the happiness of the present, defended against an uncertain future. What will happen to Martina when her mother is no longer there to fight for her against a thoughtless world? It is Berit's greatest fear. 'The worst thing that could happen would be if she were to lose any of us who are close to her . . . and that she would then be the victim of this label that says "mentally retarded". And that she would then end up in this system where people don't see the human being.'

Martina knows, too, that she has difficulties with understanding time: 'It's difficult to think into the future and into the past . . . and to think about time in general. I hate time. I'd like to live without time –

but it's not possible.' But this limitation in herself is something Martina and her mother have discovered gradually through first-hand experience, it isn't a generalization about intellectually handicapped children dumped on Martina.

And the fact of having limitations, of course, makes Martina no different from the rest of us. The point was memorably made by comedian Griff Rhys Jones on television when he admitted his own disability: he can't swim. In the sketch (shown on the BBC's 'Comic Relief 1989'), Griff squeezed in through a pub door wearing a hugh rubber lifebelt – and was told by the barman that he would have to leave. After all, rationalized the barman, if the beer barrels burst and there was a flood, Griff might be in danger as a non-swimmer and the barman would be liable for negligence . . .

It was very amusing – and not that much of an exaggeration. Children with disabilities are regularly excluded from all kinds of normal activities where their disability is obviously an irrelevance; they are often condemned to study or pursue leisure activities wherever they can get themselves accepted rather than where their talents or interests guide them. In Britain, as a result, two-thirds of disabled people live below the poverty line. Being blind (or being deaf, or being paralysed) may deprive a child of some of life's riches: being able to see the faces of the people he loves (or being able to hear music, or being able to climb mountains); but why should it also condemn him to poverty and closed doors?

The Convention on the Rights of the Child establishes the point in international law:

Article 23.1
States Parties recognize that a mentally or physically disabled child should enjoy a full and decent life, in conditions which ensure dignity, promote self-reliance, and facilitate the child's active participation in the community.

It adds that parents should be assisted, free of charge wherever possible and necessary, to give a

Prejudice and indifference in Britain mean that two-thirds of disabled people are trapped below the poverty line.

child education, health care, work and leisure opportunities,

In a manner conducive to the child's achieving the fullest possible social integration and individual development, including his or her cultural and spiritual development.

SELF-FULFILLING PROPHECIES

The trouble is, as Martina discovered, that people with certain kinds of disabilities tend to be defined in terms of their disability. Children who can't swim aren't usually referred to darkly as 'the drowners' in everyday life, but children who can't see are described regularly as 'the blind', as though that was all there was to them; children who can't hear are perceived as 'the deaf', and children who have some intellectual difficulties because of an extra chromosome are known, crushingly, as 'mongols', or even 'idiots'.

Not only does lumping together children with disabilities separate them from the able-bodied: it also falsely suggests that everyone who shares a disability is similar in every other way. But a tall, easy-going, blind girl who likes jazz is not similar to a short, tense, blind boy who likes cats and quiet.

Two disabled children will be as different from one another as any two children. But to recognize that they are different you have to see them; and you can't see them if you have shut them away.

And sometimes the able-bodied don't even look at the distinctions between one disability and another. A blind girl told me how she had been helped to fill in some forms at a bank; when she thanked the teller for her patience, she was told: 'Oh, I'm used to this sort of thing – my cousin's a cretin.' And a boy in a wheelchair said that people often don't speak to him directly but discuss him through the person pushing his wheelchair. 'It's only my arms and legs that don't work,' he protests, 'my ears and mouth and brain work perfectly well.' Sometimes he is even addressed through his dog.

These sweeping categorizations frustrate the lives of children with disabilities. The need to be seen as a unique human being is strong in all of us. But children with disabilities are often not given a chance to make themselves known as the unique human beings they are: the moment their disability is spotted – in Martina's case, from the time she was a baby in hospital – they are boxed and labelled according to the prejudices of the viewer.

And then a dangerously self-fulfilling prophecy can be set in motion. If Martina had been put in an institution at three months old instead of being at home and in a day-care centre with normal children, she might well have failed to develop her speech and her musical abilities – and that would have made it impossible for her to have been accepted at her nursery school, which in turn would have meant she wouldn't have been accepted at an ordinary primary school, and so on all through her school career: all because that first door had been closed. If we were to meet Martina after a childhood spent in institutions, instead of a childhood filled with friendly relationships with 'normal' children, what sort of a girl would we now judge her to be? And would we realize that the girl we were judging is not the real Martina, but the girl we have turned her into through the force of our narrow expectations?

Development writer Peter Adamson has described two people he met, both born deaf. One was an American, Frank Bowe, who was taught how to speak, to sign and to lip-read, so that he could communicate with hearing people almost without a hitch. He went through college as a top student and now has a successful career and a happy family life. His only sadness is that his small daughters aged one and four, get upset because they can't make him understand sound. His daughters are puzzled by this lack of responsiveness, and suspect their Daddy might be a bit stupid.

After a short while with Bowe, says Adamson, he found his attitudes to deaf people almost physically shifting. But the other encounter was quite different:

I was not introduced to Dilip Mukherjee. His brother told me about him as Dilip sat in the corner of the room staring at the floor. Like Frank Bowe, Dilip lost his hearing in early childhood. And as I listened to Frank's precise replies I remembered the strange shapeless noises which came from Dilip's mouth. He had never learned to speak.

Because of the poverty into which he was born, his family had neither the time nor the opportunity to give him the extra help he needed to overcome his hearing impairment. Deprived of stimulus since infancy, unable to read or write or find a job, Dilip has become more disabled with each passing year. Yet behind those uninquisitive eyes may have been a person with as much potential as Dr Frank Bowe. Circumstance, not impairment, has put this gulf between two men. For both are deaf, but only one is disabled.

THE WRONG BOX

Perhaps the most alarming thing of all about the power certain people have to put other people in boxes is how often their judgement is wrong. Unless parents are as strong-minded as Berit – and not that many of us are – we are likely to accept the word of the expert about our child's capabilities. But what if the expert is wrong?

Child cobbler: the glue used in shoe-making can disable a child for life.

Italy: children are a source of cheap labour in the streets and workshops of the cities.

Cleaning car windows: one of the many 'informal' jobs that children do to survive on the street. Others, like drug dealing or prostitution, are more dangerous.

Match sellers in Sri Lanka: not only a feature of Victorian times, but a reality today.

Tourists are lured to South-East Asia by 'gay guides' cataloguing boys for sexual use.

Bar girls in the Philippines – ordinary young women trying to survive are scapegoated as sinners by their customers and employers.

Aerial view of Olongapo.

Mementoes on the wall of one of the many bars in the town.

Princess and her mother Gina.

Princess and her friends play safely at the shelter while their mothers work.

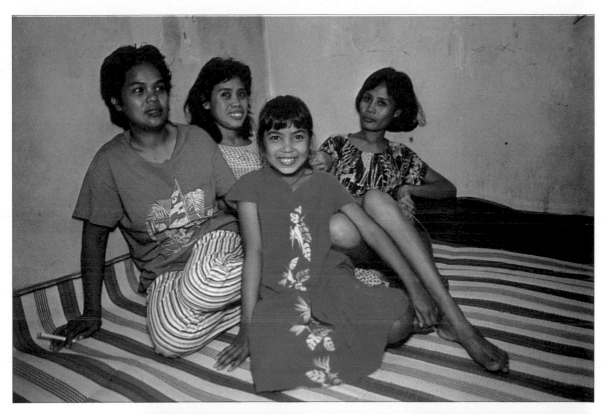

Women and girls at the Buklod night-shelter for prostitutes and their children.

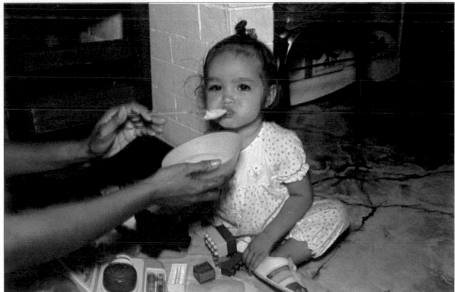

Princess often falls sick, fed by baby-sitters on bottle milk while her mother must work as a hostess in a bar.

Martina: 'I am what I am, quite simply, and no-one else.'

XXXII

Martina aged five.

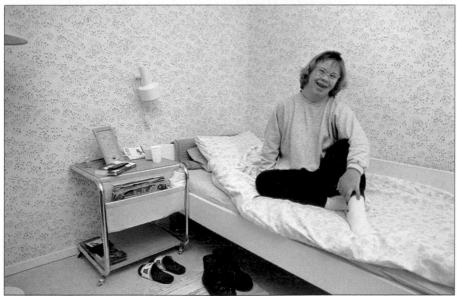

Martina in her room, where she writes about freedom and acceptance.

Martina learned to speak with the aid of music – and playing the piano is still her greatest love.

A child has a right to be seen as a human person now – not as a human-to-be when he or she becomes an adult.

*Every child is a unique human being who deserves to
be seen without preconceptions.*

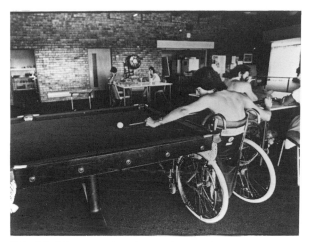

Disabled boys and girls rarely get the chance to make themselves known as the unique human beings they are.

Psychologist Dr Debbie Taylor unearthed an example of expert misjudgement coming from an institution caring for the mentally ill (another group of people who tend to be shut away by the 'normal' majority with nervous haste):

Psychologist David Rosenham and seven others – none with any history of mental illness – got themselves admitted to a mental hospital in the US, complaining that they could hear faint voices. Once admitted, they behaved normally, told everyone they felt fine, openly interviewed other patients and took copious notes. All were diagnosed schizophrenic and the hospital staff were completely taken in, interpreting all their behaviour as part of their disease: 'patient engages in writing behaviour', for instance, appears on several sets of case notes.

Appalled at his success, Dr Rosenham tried something else. He warned staff – including the psychiatrists – of another hospital that he planned to repeat the experiment, and challenged them to spot the fake patients. Now very much on the alert, the staff identified 41 fakes out of a total of 193 admissions. In fact none of Rosenham's stooges made any attempt to get into the hospital.

'The schizophrenic' has been labelled and studied as though that labelling is sound and scientific: in fact, Rosenham's experiment suggests that, in the whirling dynamic between the researcher and the patient, the only reliable fact seems to involve the expectation of the researcher: if his expectation tells him that the person before him is mentally sick, that's what he may see him to be.

The habitual relationship between the 'normal' and the 'abnormal' child in society is what needs to be challenged. What the 'normal' person thinks he sees in the other may have more to do with his own fears than with the real potential of the child before him. And yet, as long as the 'normal' have more rights than the supposedly abnormal, the right to judge them, to lock them away, to deny them their chance to develop, then the perceptual disability of the normal can seriously disable those children who had merely been impaired.

JUSTICE, NOT FAVOURS

Some people disapprove of the idea of 'positive action' or 'positive discrimination' for children with disabilities. But positive discrimination is nothing new: it has always been in operation – in favour of the able-bodied. We just haven't noticed it because it is so common. Every time a building is designed with steps, for example, instead of ramps, one group of humans is actively being favoured while another group is being disadvantaged. At a recent film and television award ceremony, a prize was awarded jointly to three people but only two came up on stage to collect the applause and the trophy; the third prize-winner was in a wheelchair and there was no ramp. Perhaps the next film the group makes will address the question 'What gives the able-bodied the right to exclude other human beings?' For the able-bodied to take note at last of the needs of disabled children to live a full life should not be regarded as doing them a special favour. If it is, then the able-bodied have been doing special favours for themselves since time immemorial.

The biggest handicap for children with disabilities is not the disability itself but the attitude of the able-bodied. The crassness with which 'normal' society turns its eyes away from people with disabilities can be devastating. When a group of young people from a residential home for people with cerebral palsy were taken out by volunteers on a day trip to the seaside, the able-bodied people at a seaside cafe told the volunteers that it was 'disgusting' that such people should be allowed out where normal people could see them. 'Who is the more seriously disabled here,' wondered an angry and distressed volunteer, 'the "normal" people, or those with cerebral palsy?'

The point is that both the 'normal' spectators and the young people with palsy had limitations, though of different kinds: the practical disability of the impaired child is one limitation but the perceptual disability of the 'normal' adult is another, greater one.

There seems to be a taboo in the minds of many 'normal' people against seeing the reality of the other, 'disabled' child before them. It is more comfortable for many of us to place an impenetrable wall between ourselves and the other, and to make generalizations or wild guesses about the nature of the child behind the wall. In this way we distance ourselves from the frightening reminder of human vulnerability – otherwise we might have to confront the fact, as Griff Rhys Jones did, that we all have disabilities, and could easily have more. It is a fact that many people would rather avoid. And yet, until we overcome our perceptual disability, the gap between one group and the other will only widen.

In Sweden, as more mothers become pregnant when they are older, more babies with Down's Syndrome are being conceived – and there are more abortions for this reason. Berit thinks these mothers

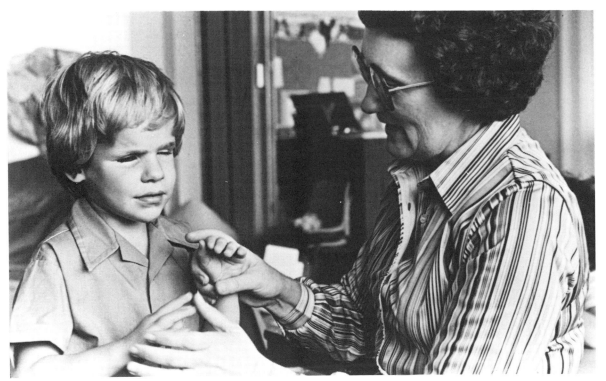

'Positive discrimination' for children with disabilities is a basic human right.

react out of fear, because they have had little real contact with an intellectually retarded person. 'They think they can be happy if they avoid handicaps and disease. But life can't be measured so easily.'

The process of discovering our own particular limitations, individual by individual, is an essential part of growing up. Psychologists like Dr Robin Skynner tell us that the process begins in infancy, when the baby discovers to his dismay that he is not the centre of the universe, summoning milk and warmth with a splendid scream. His mother, he slowly realizes, is a separate person – and gradually, as the months pass, the baby learns his own outline and realizes that an enormous amount of his world lies outside it.

Once he has got used to this dismaying lack of omnipotence, however, his limitations turn out to be quite reassuring for him; it means he is not responsible for everything – he doesn't have to keep the universe going; he need not bear the burden of infallibility. To discover the edges of our power is not inevitably to encounter misery: on the contrary, discovering who we are, outlining ourselves with our unique bumps and dents, allows us to have a refreshing sense of our own idiosyncratic reality, for no one else's outline is quite the same as ours. In this way 'normal' people learn the same lesson as the one that has to be learned by people labelled 'handicapped'.

Martina understands her unique strengths and her limitations very well. When she was asked what brought her most pleasure, she replied: 'Music . . . And having people accept me as I am – *that I am what I am, quite simply, and no one else.*'

HOW BEST TO BE RESPONSIBLE?

When Martina reached high school level, Berit managed to persuade the headmaster to put her into a special class with children who were visually, though not mentally, handicapped. The headmaster admitted his scepticism though he was willing to try it as an experiment: 'It is always an adventure to try new approaches.' In general, he said, he believed that schools for the handicapped were preferable, in which all the children are mentally retarded. But the principle embodied in the 'experiment' with Martina is now the general rule in Sweden: great pains are taken to integrate children with disabilities.

At the time of Martina's admission into school however, the headmaster wasn't alone in his scepticism. It was the prevailing attitude in the early 1980s, and there is a reasonable argument on either side: will a child with special needs get appropriate care in a school or class not geared to give it?

All children have the right to develop their potential. The Convention on the Rights of the Child establishes that in law. But the question remains: who evaluates what that potential is and how best to respond to it? How far should we lean on the side of integration – should we always go as far as Berit did, or should we linger on the side of special care, as others quite sincerely recommend?

It seems that coming down rigidly on one side or the other is not the point. The point is to be wise in the way the decision is reached: it should be arrived at through a flexible, sensitive response to the needs of the particular child in question – not through generalized assumptions about children with disabilities. True 'responsibility', as noted before, means 'response-ability': the ability to respond, rather than to offer knee-jerk reactions. Are we able to respond to each child as an individual with her or his own identity and idiosyncratic potential? Or do we think of children as identity-less lumps of clay for adults to mould as they wish, discarding lumps that seem inferior? Some people seem never to have noticed children have identities of their own. On television recently a woman dismissed the idea of child-centred care as though it had been dreamed up by a lunatic on full-moon night. Said she scornfully: '*Children* have no centres!'

As Swedish society has become more and more aware of the potential of children with disabilities, it has found ways to move along Berit's lines. It has produced another self-fulfilling cycle, but this time a benign one. In the mid-1980s, legislation was planned that would strengthen the right of the intellectually disabled to be integrated into society and Martina's experience began to be the norm rather than the exception. More and more children were allowed to live at home with their parents rather than in residential homes. Fifteen years ago, Sweden had 500 intellectually disabled children under the age of seven permanently living in institutions. Now there are less than 30.

It is important to remember, however, that closing down residential hospitals and returning children to the 'care of the community' can become a mockery if the community is unprepared and unsupported: it can simply mean that the state has abrogated its responsibility towards the children, saved itself a lot of money by closing down expensive institutions, and left families to cope if and how they can. 'Community care' can be a dishonest excuse to pass the buck to individuals. When families find they cannot cope, there is nowhere to turn. But it seems that Sweden may be taking its continuing responsibilities to children and their families seriously. National legislation underlines the state's responsibility even when children with disabilities are being cared for at home; officials are not even allowed to wait for families to ask for help – it is their duty to find out where help is needed, to offer it, and make sure it is given.

About 90 per cent of Sweden's intellectually handicapped children of pre-school age are now in ordinary pre-schools. The remaining 10 per cent attend groups housed usually in the same premises as ordinary schools so that they can mix with other children outside the classroom. 'The main principle with regard to the education of the disabled,' says a Swedish governmental document, 'is that they have the same right to education as others and in principle the right to take part in the same activities.' To maximize integration, teachers have been specially trained and technical aids have been developed with government help. 'The majority of mobility-disabled children and many pupils with defective vision and hearing now attend ordinary classes or special classes in ordinary schools.'

The children who have been least integrated have been deaf children – because 'normal' children don't know how to use sign language. Again, we could see the barrier to communication as arising from the able-bodied. Who says that talking with our vocal chords is the only 'real' way to communicate? While travelling on a bus recently I witnessed an enthusiastic – and apparently hilarious – discussion between two young people. I was longing to know what was so funny, but I didn't 'speak' sign language, and was left out by my disability.

Perhaps it's time we all learned to sign. Most schools encourage children to learn a second language: what about learning to sign as a second form of 'speaking'?

OVERTURNING THE HEALTH CARE TRIANGLE

Sweden is not only a socially progressive country: it is also small and affluent. What can be done about the millions of handicapped children in poor countries? At the start of the 1980s, there were some 200 million children with disabilities around the world – 100 million disabled by malnutrition. Another 14 million children join them every year. Can a problem of such magnitude even begin to be tackled?

The answer is yes, it can. Just one crucial adjustment in the way money is spent on health care in the poor world would go a long way towards making the problem disappear – genuinely disappear that is, not just get pushed out of sight.

At present, most of the developing world's health budget is spent on Western-style curative care. What isn't spent on training doctors and maintaining large hospitals is spent on stocking them up with expensive drugs: up to 50 per cent of Third World health budgets are spent on imported drugs. Such an expensive health care system can only be made children into society remains far down the list of health care priorities.

But we saw in chapter 5 how the upside-down triangle of education spending is being righted in some developing countries, so that primary education for all is given greater priority than advanced education for the few. The upside-down triangle of health care could be righted in the same way.

Everyone needs to be allowed to participate in the health process. 'Primary health care (PHC) for all' needs to be given priority over a system which gives high-tech health care to a privileged few and virtually nothing to the rest. PHC workers, popularly known as 'barefoot doctors', can be trained for as little as one-thousandth of the cost of training a doctor – and can be more effective in promoting general good health. These PHC workers are the guardians of simple, self-reliant, preventative methods of care. For example, they show families why it is important to eat green leaves: they're packed with vitamin A. Five cents' worth of these leaves eaten each week could save the eyesight of 250,000 children every year.

PHC workers also encourage breastfeeding; they help build cheap, safe latrines; they keep the local water supply clean; they report on family planning methods, on immunization campaigns, the use of oral rehydration salts . . . Their efforts can reduce dramatically the number of children in poor countries who become disabled or die. And PHC workers know their patients as people – they are fellow-villagers – so that children who need more advanced medical care can be spotted at an early stage. The old system misses it: if a parent has to decide alone whether to take a slightly ill child to a doctor he may well choose not to, because the doctor is miles away, the parent has no transport and must carry the sick child in the heat to a hospital where they will have to wait for hours, or travel on packed buses, and he or she will have to lose a day's pay . . . No sensible parent will inflict such a journey on a sick child except in an emergency – and yet a delay could lead to irreversible tragedy. A friendly local

In developing countries, thousands of children are still crippled by polio, as money is spent on curative medicine instead of vaccination.

available to a few people; there will never be enough money to offer it to everyone in the country.

The result is that the majority of the Third World's expensively trained doctors are to be found in the cities where their fee-paying clients live. The poor cannot afford to buy private health care – and as flimsy public health services crumble under the pressure of debt and recession, the poor are pushed further into disabling disease. In such a situation, spending money on re-integrating their handicapped

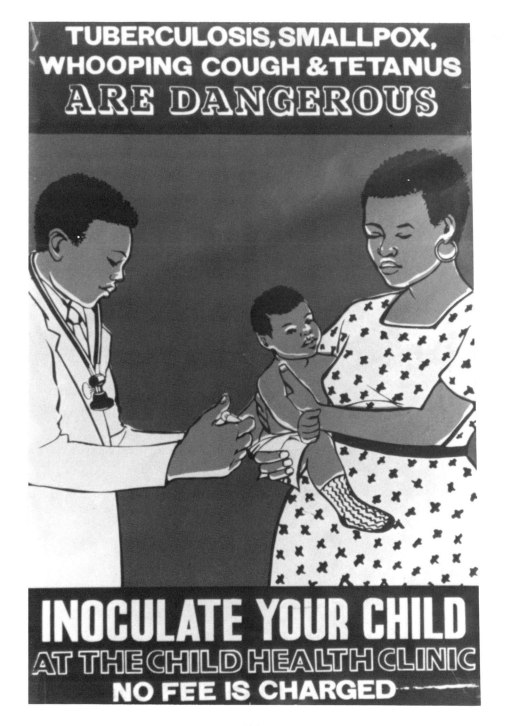

A primary health care worker shows a Jamaican mother how to stimulate her mentally handicapped baby.

PHC worker could help the parent avoid this dilemma.

Primary health care can also help the mentally ill. In China, according to psychologist Martha Livingstone and psychiatrist Paul Lowinger, each local region operates a mass mental illness and treatment programme. In Shanghai a group of cotton-weaving factories established a sheltered workshop for patients who suffered some period of mental breakdown, as well as support services for their families. This kind of support greatly reduces the recurrence rate of mental illness. One ex-mental patient described the new attitude like this: 'In the old society I would have disappeared: in the new society I can recover.'

Apart from the physical fact of better care, then,

what PHC engenders is the crucial sense of inclusion: the feeling that everyone is welcome, and has a right, to play a part in the community – and that the community is able and willing to help everyone play that part. Those who are 'imperfect' need no longer be condemned to disappear. And the others are less likely to fear imperfection when it is no longer synonymous with ostracism. They are not dependent on the expensive, hospital-based urban doctor finding time for them. Everyone can help to make themselves, their children, and their neighbours feel a healthier, happier part of the community.

Dr Alan Gilmour gives a British example of community spirit in action making a practical difference to children:

A man . . . had been imprisoned for some criminal offence, and his wife and large family moved into a house in the village. Word soon got round about their background and they found themselves shunned by most of the community. 'We don't want that criminal family mixing with our kids' was the general reaction.

Then, as Christmas approached, and plans were being made for the Christmas party for all the village children, someone mentioned this pariah family. It was Christmas, and they were lonely and unhappy-looking children, who looked as though they could do with a decent meal. This came as a rather uncomfortable suggestion at first, but shamefacedly everybody agreed it was more than time for them to do something for a family that was fatherless for no fault of their own . . . One of the villagers went round to call on the family and offer them this belated welcome. She was very distressed to find how deprived this poor family was, and how glad the mother was that something was being offered to the children.

It was quickly decided to try to do rather more . . . to make it a community responsibility to give some support to the family – a sort of collective substitute fathering. Furniture and clothing were found, and the mother was befriended and given a chance to feel that she belonged somewhere . . . Christmas presents were provided for all the children – otherwise they would have had none. They were nice children, who soon made friends, and people felt a mixture of guilt that they had ever thought or acted otherwise, and of pleasure that they were now having such a happy impact; they were very touched a little later when a letter came from a distant prison, saying how much the father appreciated his family being accepted into the community in a way that had made so much difference to their lives – and to his . . . On his discharge . . . he too came to be accepted into a community which had become that much more of a community because of this episode.

So why isn't there more emphasis on community spirit and primary health care? Not all those in positions of power over the health care of poor countries welcome the idea. Said Dr Halfdan Mahler, when he was head of the World Health Organization:

Nothing makes me scream more than people calling primary health care primitive medicine for primitive people. What they are really saying is: 'Let's continue giving hospital-based medical care for 5–10 per cent of the population – and let that siphon off 80–90 per cent of the health budget.'

A switch, then, from an ineffectual, elitist medical system to a primary health care system would allow disabled children to move from 'an old society where they disappear to a new society where they can recover'. First, some of the huge amounts of money saved could be spent on helping to integrate already-disabled children into their community – children like Gopamma. Second, supporting PHC workers would dramatically reduce the number of children who become disabled each year. And third, as disablement stopped being such a frightening spectre, the perceptual disability of the able-bodied may begin to fade.

The vast majority of disablements are not caused by acts of God or Nature: they are allowed by political neglect. The spread of most disabling disease is related to economic inequality via malnutrition, unsafe water and poor sanitation – and this political reality is within our power to alter if we wish. It has been estimated that three-quarters of the world's disease could be prevented through cheap, wide-spread primary health care – and to provide that care would cost the world only an extra 50 billion dollars per year for the next 20 years.

That is just two-thirds of what the world spends on cigarettes; half of what the world spends on alcohol; one-twentieth of what the world spends on the military. If we chose instead to spend that wealth on buying health, then almost all of the children's suffering through disabling disease would simply disappear. But somehow we have found a way to justify maiming 200 million children, plus another 14 million every year, while the money vanishes on missiles, private doctors for the ultra-rich, and an alcoholic haze.

THE CAGE DOOR OPENS

The 'ability' that empowers people the most, it seems, beyond the ability to read and write, or to walk, or to tell the time, is 'accept-ability'. But acceptability is a matter of perception. We can decide, as a world community, whether we perceive children with disabilities as acceptable members of the community or not. Of course they already *are* members of our community: the question is whether the able-bodied are going to recognize them as being so. The Convention on the Rights of the Child is an important international statement of that recognition.

And excluding children with disabilities has painful consequences not only for them: society is cutting off a valuable part of itself in an act of wilful self-mutilation. 'Martina has a lot to give,' says Berit. 'I dream about a job for her working with people, caring for the elderly, for children – she is much more gifted than we are in communicating with them.' The flip side of Martina's disability, then, is her extra ability: her openness, her sensitivity and patient, here-and-now timelessness which are as much her strengths as her limitations.

Three-quarters of the world's diseases could be prevented through low-cost primary health care.

Martina understands her paradoxical gifts. As she wrote in a poem:

I can see a black bird
   that flies through life's doors

A bird that shows its golden wings for me.
It comes from a freedom that is open,
   with unlocked doors
That bird is released from my hand
   like a freedom without wounds.

The struggle of Martina and Berit is not only the struggle of one child and one mother to be accepted into society. It reflects a change of attitude that is filtering slowly through the consciousness of the world: a new willingness to see differences in people as valuable rather than threatening. Do we want a bland oneness spreading across the planet – a human mono-culture, like the huge mono-crops covering acres upon acres of fields, where mixed crops once grew? We are beginning to be suspicious of the serried ranks of flawless tomatoes, and wonder at the flavours we have lost.

As environmentalists grapple with re-learning old lessons about the importance of diversity, we are learning the same lessons about human beings. To accept people as humans with equal rights doesn't require everyone to be the same. Uniformity is not the only way forward: unity-in-diversity, it seems, may be a better way.

Most of us have been caught up in society's addiction to perfection: we have tried hard to succeed and been afraid of being seen to fail; we have measured ourselves constantly against some abstract, half-conscious ideal and worried about not living up to it. We have rarely remembered to accept ourselves in our everyday uniqueness, our merciful differences – to celebrate the life that speaks through us just as we are. But Martina remembers: '*We are what we are, quite simply, and no one else.*'

Those of us with entrées into the magic circle of social acceptability often are, paradoxically, masters of isolation: Martina, who has been pushed out of the circle so many times, is better at intimacy. We hide our imperfections in fear behind a mask that separates us; Martina becomes strong and true by being the wounded child she is.

Martina's example shows us our right and obligation to be ourselves. 'To thine own self be true', we mutter, just before we forget and betray ourselves again by trying to be like someone else; someone nearer perfection than we. How can we create a whole-hearted relationship between ourselves and our world, if we begin by being false within ourselves?

And why is it that an intellectually disabled child can remind us of a perennial truth that we, the intellectually able ones, keep forgetting? Perhaps it is because she cannot earn acceptance into 'correct' society by our usual method: we can conceal our risky, vulnerable uniqueness, the gift of ourselves that we could have offered, by constructing a cleverly conformist front – but Martina has had to declare her differences because they are beyond concealing.

Every child has the right not to be 'perfect', as defined by some preconceived adult idea.

They could only have been concealed by shutting her out of sight in a home or a hospital, and this her mother has not allowed.

Standing on the edges of society, in full view, Martina has had to know her limitations and her strengths and accept them exactly as they are. And in her self-acceptance, she shows herself to be wiser than we have been, for she knows the value of being herself while we still hide our true selves in doubt and shame.

CONCLUSION:
LAST WORDS BEFORE ACTION

The rationalizing of inhumanity is in itself an essential part of the evil. Indeed the rationalizing can be the very essence of evil.

Bernard Nesfield-Cookson in William Blake: Prophet of Universal Brotherhood

All the children we have met in this book have been wounded in some way. Some of the children that we met fleetingly and anonymously were so badly wounded that they did not survive. They died of hunger, or disease, or war, or despairing suicide. Others lived, but so badly crippled in spirit that they were eventually locked away in gaol or locked themselves into a cage of drug-soaked, shivering fantasies. And some survived to respectable-seeming adulthood on the surface, until the needs of their own children yanked out the rage and violence of the damaged child inside.

But some children were damaged less badly — perhaps because they were wounded *and loved*, at least by someone. And loved beyond the call of easy, cheap love which turns as easily to disappointment and rejection. Those people who responded appropriately to the children were those who recognized each child's right to be seen and to develop as a unique and valuable human being, despite the veil of misconceptions shrouding him or her. Frank met social workers committed to caring for runaways despite all the negative stereotyping of street children; Martina's rights were fought for by Berit against

professional advice; Gopamma was carried to school each day by her ten-year-old brother on his back. These children whose rights were recognized not only survived their wounds so that they can now present themselves to the world as strong and worthwhile in themselves: they offer something more.

These are the children we must look to, not as the victims of society, but as among the most potent of its healers. They have learned important lessons from the painful journey between their wounding and their healing. People who feel wounded themselves don't turn away and deny the pain of others, because they feel the reality of the pain through their own wound. It is the rest of society, the overdefended, who pretend invincibility — the strong doctors who have never been helpless patients, the politicians whisked home in limousines who have never roamed the streets looking for somewhere safe to sleep, the media men looking at their watches — these are the people who can deny the agony of children victimized before their eyes, like the man who said, 'Thank heavens we are no longer faced with issues as stark as Dickens.'

What do these wounded and healing children have to say, when society finally allows them a place to speak?

'YOU CAN'T TALK THE TALK UNTIL YOU'VE WALKED THE WALK'

Gopamma, in India, says she wants to be a teacher when she grows up, helping other families to learn about the importance of immunization. Her words are likely to carry more conviction than any copy an ad-man could dream up. Frank, the big, tough, drug-dealing teenager from New York, is off the street now and pretty well off drugs. He is re-living his lost childhood, visiting the zoo, even cuddling a teddy-bear as he talks; uncovering the hurt child hidden too long beneath the tough-looking exterior. He says enthusiastically:

I would like to be a child-care worker. That's my goal, my long-term goal. I'm going to help the city. It it wasn't for the city right now I would either be dead or in gaol. It gave me a chance and I'm going to try and do what I can. Now it's time for me to help someone else who is in the same position as I am, because I don't want to see this generation go down.

Frank

Gopamma

Trudee Able-Petersen, the ex-prostitute who is now a street worker around Times Square, knows how Frank feels. She says that child prostitutes trust her because they know she's been in their shoes. For the street children who grow up into being street counsellors, the children that they help are real people, not statistics; the numbers have names, and the children they meet know the difference. Another street worker put it evocatively: 'You can't talk the talk until you've walked the walk.'

Far away from New York, in Olongapo, the Filipina prostitutes still take their children every evening to the night-care shelter at Buklod. Some go in the daytime as well to help run the centre, which they hope will be a model for many others.

They also go to the centre in order to protect it from those who see the empowerment of these young mothers and their children as a threat to the status quo.

In a letter from Buklod, Brenda Stoltzfus says that the military police come there regularly 'asking a lot of questions not relevant to the investigation they say they are doing'. The mayor, too, is suspicious of Buklod's activities. One of the mothers keeps guard, in case any of them are taken away forcibly. Despite their fear, Gina and her friends visit the shelter every day. Writes Stoltzfus: 'I see how well they are handling all of it, and feel as long as no one is physically hurt, maybe even if they are, they will come through stronger, wise and very competent. Even while I am scared for them, I feel proud of the way they are doing – their strength and commitment and acceptance. Such wonderful women!'

In Nicaragua, Manuel still spends four hours a day travelling to and from school – and his mother Elsa, who runs the house and works to make ends meet, now fits in time to study as well. Many Nicaraguan children, conscious of their good fortune, share it by teaching their parents to read and write when they come home. It's not always comfortable, switching roles like this (after all, it is parents who are traditionally supposed to teach children the skills for entering life), but pride and nerves are set aside and the effort is made by both child and parent.

And Martina? She has already had the effect of making the able-bodied people who meet her think twice about pushing children with disabilities into the shadows. She may not have 'power' in the commonly used sense, of knowing how to dominate, but she does have the power to evoke and offer gentleness and affection. Perhaps one day, as Berit dreams, Martina will work with people, looking after children or the elderly. Or perhaps she will find some other path of her own choosing; whatever it is, it is likely to involve making connections between people rather than unkind divisions. As her mother says, 'I am much more afraid of people

Martina

who are considered intelligent. They are the ones who invent atom bombs, nuclear weapons – Martina would never do such things.'

Even Princess, Gina's baby, displays her power – simply by being herself. She does not earn her right to be cared for by being clever or useful in any way: she does not justify her rights. She, perhaps more than anyone else in this book, affirms that a child is entitled to human rights by the simple virtue of being alive as a vulnerable and potent human being.

THE TURNING TIDE

And what about us? After meeting all these children, adults who read this book may feel they want to do something to stop causing children so much unnecessary suffering. We may also feel helpless, perceiving the problems too big and ourselves too powerless to make a difference. But we have two important factors on our side. One is the changing ethos surrounding children's rights: we are not fighting the tide – the tide is beginning to turn in our favour.

Though sometimes it seems like nothing will

make a tide turn, when it finally does, the effect is sudden and sweeping. All we have to do is to join that tide and add our forces, however small, to swell the flow in the new direction. The greening of attitudes to the environment provides an example. In 1980 I remember writing about the greenhouse effect, thinking despairingly that it would never be noticed in time. In spring 1988 I wrote about it again with more anxiety but scarcely more hope. Where was the serious media interest? Where was the political action?

Just three months later, every newspaper I opened had the greenhouse effect splashed across its front pages – except when the ozone hole took top billing – and every television news bulletin had one or the other as the top story. Politicians were falling over themselves to prove that they had really been 'green' all along, despite the impression they may inexplicably have given in the past. Supermarkets were wooing green consumers with everything from CFC-free deodorants to recycled toilet paper.

So I had been wrong to despair. Change can happen, and fast and worldwide. Smoking provides another example. Twenty years ago, smokers reigned supreme and taunted non-smokers to justify their non-smoking. Now smokers are found lurking in corridors, apologetic or defiant, while the non-smokers sit smugly in smoke-free rooms. A critical point seems to be reached, when the burden of proof switches sides, and an old perception suddenly gives way to a new one. While the old perception reigns, solid-sounding arguments will be found to support it; when the perception changes, these arguments dissolve and a new set of attitudes emerge.

This is what is happening now with children. The Convention on the Rights of the Child is a way in which the world begins to name its new attitude to children. And just as the change in the attitudes to the environment didn't come until the eleventh hour, when we saw that we were faced with an ecological disaster, so we have not taken serious notice of children until our treatment of them has been recognized as a worldwide tragedy – perhaps

there can never be an emergence without an emergency. But through the breakdown there has been breaking through a new awareness, as exemplified by the Convention and the network of adults working for children. The tide is on the turn.

THE WOUNDED HEALERS

Apart from the changing ethos, there is another factor acting in our favour: we may think we need to have a lot of money or influence in order to make a difference, but that's not the case. Gopamma, Frank, Martina and all the others who can 'talk the talk because they have walked the walk' are neither rich

Teaching a child with polio to swim in New York City.

nor famous. What they have is first-hand experience of what it is like to be a child whose rights have not been honoured; and experiences like this, when tempered with love and care, can lead to empathetic understanding.

Empathy is very different from pity: pity keeps us safely distanced from the object of our supposed concern. Two centuries ago, William Blake summed up the 'charitable' who indulge in pity in a single merciless verse:

> Pity would be no more
> If we did not make somebody Poor;
> And Mercy no more could be
> If all were happy as we.

But empathy doesn't want to perpetuate misery. The capacity for empathy comes from the experience of woundedness: we are linked intimately through shared suffering.

And woundedness is a quality almost all of us share with the children we have met. Most of us, at some point in our own lives, have known the experience of being deeply hurt and abandoned. We know what it is like to try, time and again, to be accepted; to risk betraying our true selves in order to be loved – and yet to fail. Through this wound, we can understand the pain that children suffer.

Some people choose to express their empathetic feelings for children by helping them directly – by fostering a rejected child; visiting a child in a detention centre and becoming a positive life-line to the outside world; working for fairer education or health care for all children, or for the integration of children with disabilities; working with support groups for children who have been assaulted, or being a telephone link for parents who feel at the end of their tether.

Others help children indirectly, by approaching adults who have power over children's lives: persuading banks to reconsider the terms of their loans to poor countries; insisting that politicians spell out exactly how the policies they implement will affect children. The people who press for large-scale political or social change like this may find themselves able to help far more children than they could hope to help one at a time.

Still others look imaginatively at their jobs as new avenues for raising public awareness about the needs and rights of children. Who would have expected a decade ago that pop stars would stand as public consciences, as Bob Geldof did? Other people raise awareness in the community groups to which they belong, or they form groups around an issue they feel strongly about. One group of women who wanted to deter sex tours went to the airport and met the tourists as they disembarked, waving placards to show they knew what the men were up to. The customers' embarrassment was enormous – they are unlikely to want to go through that again.

PULLING BACK THE CURTAIN

The women at the airport did something very important. They broke through the sense of an 'open secret' – the sort of secret which everyone half-knows about, but feels uncomfortable about investigating. It is especially strong where sexual secrets are concerned, which is one reason why the sexual exploitation of children has gone on for so long. We are afraid to get involved – afraid to meet hostility from the powerful keepers of the secret, or embarrassed that our own dark secrets may be pulled out of closets, or we may simply have a prickling sense that we have touched an area that is taboo: and so we back away.

This is the taboo that allows evil to be perpetuated; fear holds the rationalizations for evil in place. Whole cities like Olongapo, as we have seen, can operate a collective taboo, repressing those who refuse to comply with it. And families where children are sexually abused, as we have also seen, are also protected by denial and taboo: few people want to know that there are children being abused within the family walls. Money, too, often has a protective

Child prostitute in Bombay: time to confront the abuse of children worldwide.

mystique woven around it. In fact, anything that a powerful person wants strongly to keep hidden and under his control tends to have a heavy black curtain around it, which others are led to believe they draw aside at their peril.

Because most of us are so intimidated, the powerful get to keep their secrets – and the children go on being victimized behind the curtain. It is this taboo that is the greatest barrier to change; it seals eyes and ears. As long as we can deny our agonies and the agonies that other children are going through, we can turn away and not act. Even if we are influential, or have money, or intellectual prowess, we will not use those resources for helping children.

But once we begin to uncover our own wounds and grieve over them, once we begin to mourn for the innocents we were, who were robbed of our rights before we could defend ourselves, then nothing else will seem as urgent as staunching the pain of other children and defending their rights. Like the women at the airport, we will be ready to come out from behind our masks of sophistication, and act on our responsibilities to children simply and directly.

STANDING ON A SOAP-BOX

Once our will is behind limiting children's pain to that which is necessary and unavoidable, we will be ingenious in discovering ways to prevent unnecessary pain; and we will be too sensitized to fall for rationalizations that prolong unnecessary suffering.

We will not accept, for instance, that it is necessary to starve childen in order to pay interest on debts to people who live in luxury.

Are we prepared to put children first?

We will not accept that it is necessary for a child to die of diseases that are preventable for the price of a packet of cigarettes – and that a million children each month must die like this. We will not accept that as many must be crippled and pushed out of a full experience of life's joys.

We will not accept that children may be used for the sexual gratification of adults, whether they are forced to do so by economic inequality or by family demands.

We will not accept that children may be bought and sold like pieces of property.

We will not accept that children should work as slaves, and neither have time nor energy to play, nor to benefit financially from their labour.

We will not accept that children should go to war as soldiers, nor that they should be tortured and mutilated if they refuse.

We will not accept that children whose parents reject them will have nowhere to go but the street.

These realities exist today because enough adults consider them acceptable: the consensus of adult opinion has allowed them to continue. It is this consensus that we must now reject, to build a new consensus that will enforce the rights of children.

Most of the children deprived of their rights today have no means to plead their cause. Their voices will never be heard; we will never see the agony on their faces. Every hurt child whom we do see or hear represents a million, or ten million, or a hundred million other children, fading or dying. But through the children that we have met in these pages, and the wounded child within us, we have borne witness to their pain. Will we keep burying that pain in our hearts – or will we speak out?

Recommended reading

The State of the World's Children Report (Oxford University Press, annual).
Anti-Slavery Society, Continuing series on child labour.
Agnelli, S., *Street Children* (Weidenfeld and Nicolson, 1986).
Bishop, G., *Innovations in Education* (Macmillan, 1986).
Campbell, B., *Unofficial Secrets* (Virago, 1988).
Christian Aid, *Banking on the Poor* (Christian Aid, 1988).
Cleese, J. and Skynner, R., *Families and How to Survive Them* (Methuen, 1984).
Ennew, J., *The Sexual Exploitation of Children* (Polity Press, 1986).
Franklin, R., *The Rights of Children* (Basil Blackwell, 1986).
Fyfe, A., *All Work and No Play* (TUC/UNICEF, 1985).
George, S., *A Matter of Life and Debt* (Penguin, 1988).
Gilmour, A., *Innocent Victims* (Michael Joseph, 1988).
Glaser, D. and Frosh, S., *Child Sexual Abuse* (Macmillan, 1988).
Greer, G., *Sex and Destiny* (Secker and Warburg, 1984).
Hoyles, M., *The Myth of Childhood* (Journeyman, 1989).
Miller, A., *The Drama of Being a Child* (Virago, 1987).

Picture credits

The author and publisher are grateful to the following for their kind permission to reproduce illustrations on the following pages: Ellen Aanesen 104, 106–8, 110, 112, 114–18, 120; The Anti-Slavery Society 95–6, 101 (photo: Sumanta Banerjee); The Anti-Slavery Society/TESCRO 88–9; Aspect Picture Library/Mike Wells xiv; Christian Aid/Chris Steele-Perkins 42, 47; Peter Claesson 122, 126, 138, 142b; Colorific!/Joy Wolf 20; Danish Folk High School Association 79; Dante Fasciolo 91; Format/Brenda Prince 82; Impact/Christopher Cormack 18; International Labour Office 7; ILO/J.P. Laffont/Sygma 92; Richard Keefe 14, 17, 22–3, 28, 30, 32, 34–6, 142t, 143; Rick McKay, Cox Newspapers, Washington Bureau 98–9; Magnum 5, Magnum/Steve Curry 9; Magnum/Stuart Franklin 11, 71; Magnum/Leonard Freed 16; Magnum/Eugene Richards 25–6; Magnum/Eugene Smith 44; Magnum/Rene Burri 62; Magnum/Sebastia Salgado 64; Magnum/Ferdinando Scianna 65; Magnum/Peter Marlow 78, 109, 140; Magnum/Cornell Capa 83; Magnum/David Hurn 127; Magnum/Gideon Mendel 147; National Museum of Labour (photo: Anti-Slavery Society) 102; Network/Mike Goldwater 8; Network/Mike Abrahams 46; Oxfam 41; Panos Pictures/Martin Adler 13; Panos Pictures/Peter Charlesworth 38; Panos Pictures/Wendy Wallace 43; Panos Pictures/Paul Harrison 54; Panos Pictures/Sean Sprague 55; Panos Pictures/Bror Karlsson 73; Panos Pictures/Mark Edwards 75, 133, 146; Panos Pictures/Mark Adler 149; Rapport Photo Agency/Margaret Olah 129–30; Manuel Ripoll 68, 72; Berit Schaub 124; David Springbett 50, 52–3, 59–60, 66; UNICEF 57; UNICEF/Reynolds 1; UNICEF/Jonathan Weinberger 2; UNICEF/Jacques Danois 4; UNICEF/Bruce Thomas 40; UNICEF/T.S. Satyan 76; UNICEF/Claudio Edinger 94; UNICEF/Maggie Black 134; UNICEF/Maxwell 135; UNICEF/Heidi Larson 137; UNICEF/Tom Marotta 144; UNICEF Italia/C.I. Crocevia 86; UNRWA 39; United Nations/Jean-Pierre Laffont 103; Glen Williams 70.

The author and publisher are grateful to the following for their kind permission to reproduce colour plates: Ellen Aanesen XXVIII–XXXI; Aslak Aarhus I, XXIVb; Sverre Aurstad IIIb; Trygve Bølstad IVb, XVIIt; Peter Claesson XXXII, XXXIIIb–XXXIV;

Colorific!/John Launois/Black Star VIIb; Colorific!/Wesley Bocke/J.B. Pictures XIIt; Colorific!/G. Hiller/Wheeler Pictures XIIb; Format/Jeremy Matthews XXIIIb, XXXV; Ole Bernt Froshaug XXI; Impact/Christopher Pillitz V; Impact/Mark Cator IXt; Impact/ Martin Black Xt; Richard Keefe XI, XIII–XV, XVIIb; Inge Lie II; Magnum/Steve McCurry VI; Magnum/Ferdinando Scianna VIIt; Magnum/Eli Reed Xb; James Natchway XXIIt; Mike Okoniewski/Liaison IVt; Panos Pictures/Jeremy Hartley XVI; Panos Pictures/Paul Harrison XXIV; Panos Pictures/John Delorme XXXVI; Manuel Ripoll XXIIb, XXIIIt; Berit Schaub XXXIIIt; David Springbett IXb, XVIII–XX; Frank Spooner XXVIIb; Frank Spooner/Gamma VIII, XXVIIt; UNICEF IIIt; UNICEF Italia/ C.I. Crocevia XXIVt, XXVI.

Cover illustrations: (front) photograph: UNICEF/Kiloran Howard; (back) photographs by Ellen Aanesen (middle, right), Peter Claesson (bottom, right), Richard Keefe (left & right, top) and David Springbett (bottom, left).

INDEX

Index by Ann Hall